Kabbalah and Art

Kabbalah

and Art

LÉO BRONSTEIN

Published by the Brandeis University Press

Distributed by the University Press of New England

Hanover, New Hampshire and London, England 1980

Copyright© 1980 by Eleanor L. Wolff

All Rights Reserved

Library of Congress Cataloging Card Number 78-63585

International Standard Book Number 0-87451-163-1

Printed in the United States of America

Library of Congress Cataloging in Publication data
will be found on the last printed page of this book.

The present volume is the first to be published by the
Brandeis University Press under the auspices of the
Brandeis University Léo Bronstein Memorial Fund,
established soon after the death of Léo Bronstein
on June first, 1976, for the publication of
his several posthumous works.

Acknowledgments

ITS AUTHOR DEAD, this book survives because of the Brandeis University Léo Bronstein Memorial Fund—Brandeis' Dean Jack S. Goldstein and Vice President David Steinberg, who set it up and with every kindness and courtesy administer it, and the friends, family and former colleagues and students who have contributed to it, some of them so generously. Robert Pomerance, who studied with Léo at the Asia Institute, guided us as a friend through the period of negotiation. Three former Brandeis students of Léo's—or rather, four, for Eric Zafran, Curator of the Chrysler Museum in Norfolk, Virginia, has lent support from the first—have given time and encouragement: Annika Barbarigos of the Institute of Fine Arts, New York University; Laurin Raiken, Assistant Professor, School of the Arts, New York University; Arnold Spicehandler, Field Service Director, B'nai B'rith. Arthur Polonsky, Associate Professor of Fine Arts, Boston University, gave to us and to the book, in memory of his old friend, the ink drawing *The Song And The Space*. We owe most grateful thanks to Léo's former colleague at Brandeis, Professor Walter Spink of the Department of History of Art, University of Michigan, in general for his warm interest in this as in Léo's other works, and in particular for his help toward procuring the Indian illustrations. Léo's former publisher, Thea Wheelwright, has helped beyond the call of duty with the editing.

It is with me, as the owner of Léo Bronstein's posthumous work, that responsibility for errors and omissions must rest.

Not one book of Léo Bronstein's but has struck the note of elegy.

vi
Acknowledgments

Now it is our turn. Professor Richard Edwards, Assistant Professor Abigail Rosenthal and Professor Emeritus Henry Rosenthal have given more than prefatory words: they have spoken for us all.

In this place it seems fitting to light, as it were, a candle to Narcis Serradell I Pascual, Léo's foster-father in name and deed.

November 1978   *Eleanor L. Wolff*

Contents

Notes on Illustrations

and Related Material. Photograph by John and Susan Huntington.

Pope-Hennessy, in *Sienese Quattrocento Painters* (Oxford, Phaidon Press, 1947), says that this panel—along with one in the Vienna Kunstakademie—forms part of a predella containing scenes from the legend of the Augustinian saint, Nicholas of Tolentino.

Foreword

THOSE WHO READ THIS BOOK and have known Léo Bronstein will always see him in its pages, will recognize his style, its initial seeming obscurity, but a style that with persistence reveals the ease of a mind that knows its truth and sees it in a bewildering variety of places —or perhaps more accurately in the light of place-time metaphors, especially the metaphors of art.

It is a book about art which is itself a work of art. It is not easy. It requires reading, re-reading and re-reading. Its brevity allows this. *Kabbalah and Art* is noteworthy for its condensation and, accordingly, its own self-affirmation: "Art is not expansion, it is reduction." Its condensation is filled with the unexpected, the oblique (and thus uniquely forceful) approach to reality. Kabbalah is about spirituality as art is about spirituality, both in a unique way: "It is more spiritual to be with the mysteries of the body than with the mysteries of the spirit." What Kabbalah says is also what art says: in Dosso Dossi, in India, in Dégas, in Klee, in Picasso. It is unashamedly about mysticism: "a visionary —a visual—experience through and through." And rather like a mystery—a detective story—an impossible ending, the tough accusation: "Dégas, you, the Jew-hater, you were the painter of the Jewish mystical vision . . ."

Kabbalah and Art is scholarly. It is documented. But it is the creation of a unique mind. It is a book written with brevity and tenderness about art's meaning. It will help us see—and live—better.

November 1978   *Richard Edwards*

Foreword

LÉO BRONSTEIN'S BOOK has this thesis: (1) that in the thick overlay of categories of the Kabbalah there is contained an epistemology, or theory of knowledge; (2) that that epistemology offers postulations about how to know the fundamentals of existence: God, the world, and mankind: (3) that man, in his ethical life of good and evil and in his passion for visionary understanding, and the world, in its germination of structure, both exhibit an equipoised dialectic of the masculine and the feminine, the name for which is "Presence" or *Shekhinah*; (4) that art, in its history and in its born-again incarnations as this painting, this vision, or that, is the Kabbalah itself (the "same as itself"), knowing, knowledgeable, dazzling, and explosive of spirit.

The exposition of this thesis, sometimes rhapsodic but always steadfast, shows Léo Bronstein homing in on a redoubt of the mind that has been his life-long goal, as author, creative teacher and illuminist. That redoubt, or perhaps shelter, is where art and wisdom dwell together, altogether confident of one another's support. A vast knowledge of art, and experience of it, enables Léo to move with an almost native authority through the baroque thickets of kabbalistic concept and Hassidic story; and an uncompromising empathy with the passion of Kabbalah enables him to turn the power of tenderness and revivification on the great iconographic familiars of western art to redeem them to a meaning beyond the walls, and into the troubled souls of men.

Those who knew Léo will recover in this climactic chapter of his sojourn a splinter of his spirit. Those who did not may well recover in this commentary a fragment of themselves.

October 1976   *Henry M. Rosenthal*

About
Léo Bronstein

LÉO BRONSTEIN WAS BORN IN AUGUSTOVO, Russia (now Poland). He studied literature and philosophy at the University of Madrid between the years 1920 and 1923, and subsequently studied philosophy and fine art in Paris. In 1932 he was awarded the degree of Docteur de l'Université de Paris at the École de Psychologie and the École des Professeurs of the Sorbonne, working chiefly under the direction of Henri Foçillon. From this period come his first two books, *Lutte et réconciliation: Essai sur la manifestation du réel dans l'art*, and *Altichiero: L'Homme et son oeuvre*, a study of Italian art in the fourteenth century which was his doctoral thesis.

He came to this country in 1932 and became first Research Associate and then Associate Professor at the Iranian Institute of Art and Archaeology (later, the Asia Institute), teaching the history of Near Eastern art, the social and economic history of Iran, and advanced and intermediate courses in the Russian language. There he was also Director of the Documentary Survey, which summarized and catalogued the documentary material in European languages bearing on the history of Iranian art and culture. The Survey subsequently passed from the Institute to the Fogg Art Museum of Harvard University. To the Asia Institute period belongs his next book, *El Greco*.

In 1952 he joined the faculty of Brandeis University, retiring in 1967, as Professor Emeritus in the Fine Arts and Near Eastern Civilization. He was a celebrated teacher, lecturing to packed auditoriums. After his last class at Brandeis, his students organized a surprise outdoor party and picnic that has since become a celebratory event (Léo Bronstein day or—in 1978—weekend) each year at Brandeis.

The books of his last years were *Fragments of Life, Metaphysics and Art* and *Five Variations on the Theme of Japanese Painting.*

On June 1, 1976, Léo Bronstein was killed accidentally by a motorcyclist in Strasbourg, where he had gone on his way to see the Gruenewald "Crucifixion" in Colmar. Of the additional manuscripts not yet published at the time of his death, *Kabbalah and Art* was his last (most recently completed) work.

Léo Bronstein was a member of a notable musical family. His brother is Rafael Bronstein, the violinist and teacher of musicians. His niece is Ariana Bronne, the concert violinist. His grandniece is Nanette Glushak, the ballerina.

What is difficult about describing the man is to account, in a few short words, for the look on the faces of his near relations, students, colleagues and other friends at the memorial meeting organized by Brandeis University. His mourners looked to me like abandoned orphans. Since they were after all an élite gathering—certainly cultivated, worldly and resourceful beyond the average—one would have to suppose that the "protection" they felt Léo gave them was woven of no ordinary stuff. It was an emotional, moral and aesthetic protection, woven of the finest threaded alchemical gold. People took Léo's presence in their lives as a sign that their fondest hopes were profoundly justified; and likewise a sign that their worst terrors were—with great finality and truth—understood. Léo was as good a concretization of the rabbinic legend of the 36 whose righteousness is the secret support of the world as most of us are likely to encounter. His vision and passion seemed to maintain the world as a bearable condition. I thought there was ample reason for the remark of one of the nearer mourners to me: "To tell you the truth, I can't live without him."

To tell the truth, we don't have to live without him. We can (now at last) read and (slowly) absorb his books, in their conjoined significance. I felt no need to do this while he was around. It seemed superfluous to read Léo when one could see him and talk to him. I see with enormous interest and relief that there is—through his books—the possibility of continuing to learn from him now that he is physically gone.

Kabbalah and Art is a work for the seeker, rather than a work for the conventional reader. It is perhaps the densest and most impressionistic of Léo's works. It may be best read in conjunction with some of the more discursive earlier works, such as *Fragments of Life, Metaphysics and Art*. The sincere seeker will gain from a meditative reading of *Kabbalah and Art*, however, unmistakable glimpses of a seeker and thinker of great stature who is traveling down a rich vein of existence, on which he has already traveled very far and seen much more than the average seeker. What he has seen and known has evidently given Léo Bronstein the courage of *earned* originality.

I would try to paraphrase the thesis of *Kabbalah and Art* as follows: Justice alone is not enough; the ethical alone is never enough. There is in the ethical an exclusionary character which is *at once* and pervasively made up for and compensated by the art-image. And this compensatory soothing redistribution of affect and percept is a characteristic of reality itself. It is not a projection or mere wish about reality, for visual art is not a merely human wish projected on the impassive material medium; it is an expression of the indispensably feminine side of reality itself, which Kabbalah calls "mercy." Mercy seems to flow into the dry places made by justice, as sea water flows back into a pit dug furiously by a child in the sand.

What is Jewish about this hypothesis (or visionary assertion) of the intertwining of art-image and ethical concept, mercy and justice, is perhaps its refusal of reification. An art-image may be, by what Léo Bronstein calls "substitution," a point of ingathering for the Infinite. But no single art-image (such as the image of Christ) may preempt the field of the Infinite and subordinate the other art-images to itself. There is, then, no exclusive "stone" that was first rejected and then "made head of the corner." Léo Bronstein takes the Jewish intention—in its Kabbalistic expression—to be world-pervasive. He does so for all kinds of reasons, some of which I can only conjecture or impute to him, on the basis of the clues in *Kabbalah and Art*. Perhaps the Jewish intention is one of iconoclastic interiority, and therefore world-pervasive. Perhaps it is also conceptual, and therefore world-pervasive. Certainly it is historical and in quest of justice, and therefore absolutely influential. Perhaps because, by nature and vocation, the Jewish intention accepts and absorbs the actual, it seeps through other cultures and unavoidably pervades the world. Others have thought so, about the Jewish intention, for these and other reasons. In *Kabbalah and Art*, Léo Bronstein seems not so much to *think* the Jewish intention world-pervasive, even of the most remote and un-Jewish art-images, as to *see* that it is so, and to begin his story from there. What is religious about this insight is the attribution of such pervasive intentions not only to the single relentless culture of the Jews, but also to the Creator, and to the Creation as the Creator's reflection-absorbed.

I have known Léo Bronstein almost all my life. He was there to look me over through the visitor's window pane at the hospital where I was born. In my childhood I was to listen, uncomprehending but fascinated, to the conversations between my father, the late Professor Henry M. Rosenthal, and Léo, and I think that I began to study philosophy so that I could understand those conversations.

But there are also many aspects and reflections of Léo which are signs of the singular environment that he created. The stories he knew! The things that happened to him! The unsentimental aphorisms: "The world prefers a murderer to a petty-petty thief." (And the world, he felt, was in this false-fastidiousness mistaken.) Or, on higher education: "The kids are forced—forrrced—to study sublime matters. Sublime-matters! It is wonderful!" Or the mock-musical refrain, condensing the accents of the many languages he spoke and read, with which he'd punctuate some droll anecdote or narrative account of human insufficiency: "What do I know?" he would say. "How can I judge?" Meaning that he *could* judge, and he did know, but that that fact was not all-important.

When he was a younger man, he was very handsome, and he dressed incomparably well, all his life, in what may have been the Catalan style of his youth. He loved parties and "good-times," as he called them—yet in the years I knew him there was hardly a day that was not partly spent in giving physical care to some elderly, enfeebled, or otherwise handicapped person.

When he was in the middle of his life, crossing the Atlantic as he often used to do at the time when my parents first knew him, a couple approached him on shipboard, apologizing for their intrusion but explaining that they had recently returned from India where they had been studying with a Master, that they recognized in him another Master, and would be grateful if he would permit them to study with him, to teach them what he knew. Léo laughed, of course, and said that he did not know anything.

Another time—in my childhood now—he came up to visit my family at the summer place we rented in New Jersey. It happened that our landlady was a theosophist, in addition to being a rather strong-minded, energetic and practical person. "Is that Léo?" she asked. "Why, he's an Enlightened being." How, she was asked, could she tell? "It's obvious," our landlady replied cryptically. "I can see his halo."

I think there were many people who saw in him a master, though not in the dogmatic or hieratic sense, and saw or thought they saw his halo, though not in the physical sense.

November 1978   *Abigail L. Rosenthal*

Publications of Léo Bronstein

Lutte et réconciliation: Essai sur la manifestation du réel dans l'art, Paris, Felix Alcan, 1927

Altichiero: L'Homme et son oeuvre, Paris, J. Vrin, 1932

El Greco, New York, Harry N. Abrams, 1950

Fragments of Life, Metaphysics and Art, New York, Bond Wheelwright, 1953

Five Variations on the Theme of Japanese Painting, Freeport, Maine, Bond Wheelwright, 1969

Kabbalah and Art, Waltham, Mass., Brandeis University Press, Distributed by the University Press of New England, 1979

The chapters "Decorative Woodwork of the Islamic Period" and "Enamel," in *A Survey of Persian Art*, ed. Arthur Upham Pope–Phyllis Ackerman (London and New York, Oxford University Press) Vol. III, 1937

"Research Program of the Institute—The Documentary Survey,"
Bulletin of the American Institute for Persian Art and Archaeology,
Vol. I, no. 6 (1934), 16–17; IV, 3 (1936), 153–58; V, 1 (1937), 42–46

"Space Forms in Persian Miniature Composition," *Bulletin of the
American Institute for Persian Art and Archeology,* Vol. IV, no. 1 (1935),
15–28

"Some Historical Problems Raised by a Group of Iranian Islamic
Potteries," *Bulletin of the American Institute for Persian Art and
Archeology,* Vol. V, no. 3 (1938), 225–35

Kabbalah and Art

TO MY READER. PERSON TO PERSON

I

Prologue

CHORUS MYSTICUS

Alles Vergängliche
Ist nur Gleichnis;
Das Unzulängliche,
Hier wird's Ereignis;
Das Unbeschreibliche,
Hier ist's gethan;
Das Ewigweibliche
Zieht uns hinan.

End of Goethe's *Faust II* [1]
(to be read anew)

Once in your life—or twice, or more, fatigue allowing it, you must have met an object of life and of creation, old or young, that was your meeting with friendship. A prophetic meeting: the meeting with your spirituality.

*   *   *

Spirituality: to know, that inside and outside all life and all creation, success is not the contrary of failure; that the two worlds are two dimensions, but not contrary to each other. Success is to be the achieve-

I. DOSSO DOSSI: *St. John the Baptist.*

ment of a goal known, open, given. Failure, achievement of a goal not known yet, hidden and to be discovered.

Friendship is to know this. Prophecy is about this. Spirituality means this.

*   *   *

Thus it was one day, when passing through the princely rooms of the Pitti Palace in Florence, my eye—sliding away from the too forcibly admired and immutable works of the Great, over the picture-glutted walls of the Not-so-great—met there, crowded high up, irreverentially lost, this very friendship, this prophecy and this very spirituality: the Giaconda-like erect half-figure of St. John the Baptist, made one with the Emilian landscape (*Plate 1*), painted with magic intentions (such, *ab initio*, as Friendship had sealed it there for me—a neuro-electronic chain of reactions-responses along memory's feedback deeds: smell-surprise=bliss-and-fear in a handicapped child, the bliss-and-fear of green-into-greener, the bluer blue in that landscape-glance: handicapped child's bliss-and-fear, opaque, liquid, gaseous, and the metaphysical protection already in it), by the sixteenth-century Ferrarese, Dosso Dossi.[2]

*   *   *

In my memory's feedback deeds I saw floating Degas' convinced and obsessive motto: *Le beau est un mystère.*

*   *   *

What is Dosso's *mystère*, his-my friendship? Music. And—not side-by-side with, but *via* music, Woman.

Music:

That which makes me, a solid, opaque, moving and serene being—me or Ararat's summit at the Deluge—become, fire doing this, a restless liquid, transparent, directed, mobile—me or deluge or tear, or ocean or stream—and then, fire increased, become the gaseous, translucidly light, fulfilled, agitated and explosive me, the same me, the primeval, elemental atom-gas, the bearer of astrophysics' creation-bang!, a new being, solid, opaque and serene, severe-and-merciful.

Music. The Giorgionesque Venetian music-secret in Dosso Dossi. Music, so to speak (*Plates* 2, 3, 4, 5).

*   *   *

2. DOSSO DOSSI: *Melissa.*

3. DOSSO DOSSI: *Circe and Her Lovers in a Landscape.*

4. GIORGIONE: *The Tempest.*

5. TITIAN: *The Concert.*

So to speak, I say. For: "Words, words, words!" as, severely and merci-fully, the Poet said long ago. And yet, as another long after him wanted it: *Poésie n'est pas faite avec des idées mais avec des mots.*

Still, in both, the multi-valent intention remains the same: Shakespeare's and Mallarmé's arrested despair of limitations and of insufficiency—"words, words, words!" *words around ideas*—and, to-gether with it, their transfer of such a despair into the hope-full act of creation itself: their own words—their words' plunge into the pleni-tude of touch-smell-taste-vision-sound-gesture-idea, *the total word.*

Poet's plenitude. Poet's plunge into and emergence from (his coming out, one with it) the sound-genesis of man's most ancient meditation: the Hindu *Sabdā,* the in-sound, total, of all beginnings and embodiments, with no beginnings, no ends in it; more precisely or closely, the pre-spoken speech, the in-sounding total sound-word, the Hebrew letter-sound *Yod,*[3] this "cause of causes," this prophetic pleni-tude, of the primeval creation's bang *ex nihilo,* ultimate meditation of thinkers-kabbalists of old, the sixteenth-century Cordovero in Galilean Saphed, the thirteenth-century Isaac the Blind of Pasquières, Azriel of Gerona, Abulfia, Gikadilla and others in Provence, Catalonia and Castile.

Such, in our own watchful and impatient century, and among its earnest thinkers—helpers—the plenitude of their in-out despair, the plenitude of in-out insufficiency, and their search for issue.

Despair.

In Ludwig Wittgenstein: "Philosophy is a battle against the be-witchment of our intelligence by means of language."[4]

"The results of philosophy are the uncovering of one or another piece of plain nonsense and of bumps that the understanding has got by running its head against the limits of language. These bumps make us see the value of the discovery!"[5]

And ". . . any interpretation still hangs in the air along with what it interprets, and cannot give it any support. Interpretations by them-selves do not determine meaning."[6]

And "My aim is to teach you to pass from a piece of disguised nonsense to something that is patent nonsense."[7]

"Language is a labyrinth of paths. You approach from *one* side and know your way about; you approach the same place from another side and no longer know your way about."[8]

And: Despair's in-out: "But we *understand* the meaning of a word when we hear or say it; we grasp it in a flash, and what we grasp in this way is surely something different from the 'use' which is extended in time!"[9] "Remember that the look of a word is familiar to us in the same kind of way as its sound."[10]

"What is your aim in philosophy? To shew the fly the way out of the fly-bottle."[11]

"But isn't it our *meaning* it that gives sense to the sentence? (And here, of course, belongs the fact that one cannot mean a senseless series of words.) And 'meaning it' is something in the sphere of the mind. But it is also something private! It is the intangible *something* only comparable to consciousness itself.

"How could this seem ludicrous? It is, as it were, a dream of our language."[12]

". . . 'When we mean something, it's like going up to someone, it's not having a dead picture (of any kind).' We go up to the thing we mean.

"'When one means something, it is oneself meaning'; so one is oneself in motion. One is rushing ahead and so cannot also observe oneself rushing ahead. Indeed not." Yet: "Yes: meaning something is like going up to someone."[13]

And: "'I noticed that he was out of humour.' Is this a report about his behaviour or his state of mind? ('The sky looks threatening'; is this about the present or the future?) Both; not side-by-side however, but about the one *via* the other."[14]

"Though—one would like to say—every word has a different character in different contexts, at the same time there is *one* character it always has: a single physiognomy. It looks at us.—But a face in a *painting* looks at us too."[15]

"The evolution of the higher animals and of man, and the awakening of consciousness at a particular level. The picture is something like this: Though the ether is filled with vibrations the world is dark. But one day man opens his seeing eye, and there is light."[16]

"Again: I do not 'observe' what only comes into being through observation. The object of observation is something else."[17]

"'Now I am seeing *this*,' I might say (pointing to another picture, for example). This has the form of a report of a new perception.

"The expression of a change of aspect is the expression of a *new*

perception and at the same time of the perception's being unchanged."[18]
        "We find certain things about seeing puzzling, because we do not find the whole business of seeing puzzling enough."[19]

And no contradiction should be seen, I think, between this vision of despair's battle with *both* despair and hope, in later Wittgenstein, and his earlier but definitive legacy as summarized for us by Bertrand Russell: "Every language has . . . a structure concerning which, *in the language*, nothing can be said, but . . . there may be another language dealing with the structure of the first language, and having itself a new structure, and . . . to this hierarchy of languages there may be no limit."[20]

The plenitude of inter-translatability of all languages—the languages of tongue, eye, ear, hand, etc.—and the presence of loss in it:

a) the unforgivable loss of solitude (where a word is a word, a gesture is a gesture, an idea is an idea),

b) the mystery of that very loss being gain—the mystery of solidarity in it, the mystery of solitude-solidarity.

And all poets—the poets of words, of sounds, of gesture, of abstraction and of touch and smell—know: that all mystery, the secret of a secret, is that which is when where and what it is and not any disturbed else. Ancient wisdom's invention, today's existentialist cliché: everything is nothing, has the nothing in it, for without this nothing everything would not be anything.

Shelley's "To defy Power, which seems omnipotent; . . . to hope till Hope creates / From its own wreck the thing it contemplates."

                    ⋆   ⋆   ⋆

. . . The secret of Dosso Dossi: the word music and—not "side-by-side" with but *"via"* the word music and *via* the word man in it, the word Woman in it.

                    ⋆   ⋆   ⋆

So to speak, I said.

"And to imagine a language means to imagine a form of life."[21] Wittgenstein interrupts again here, threatens and helps those who need such help. "I shall also call the whole, consisting of language and the actions into which it is woven, the 'language game'."[22]

The woman. In Dosso Dossi. Perhaps in all that is meant by creation here. (The giving and bearing of life, the giving and bearing it to death.) The Woman. A word and a discovery. But discovery is always the discovery also of the *else* in the discovered. Here as plenitude, as continuity—without distances in it: the "else" of what is far—in time and in space—and what is close, is the same. Such is the confession of a poet: the secrecy and the silence of the poignant in it. The same-else in it.

The Woman. Not Graves's White Goddess (but this too); not even the man's pain-quenching desire of the perfect curve, the sorceress's perfect breasts—male's existential plenitude. (But this too, of course.) Not even depth-psychology's archetypal, Faustian descent into the Mothers' abode and Faust's depth-ascension back to that pain-quenching fulfillment of plenitude—Goethe's beautiful Helen. (Yet this too.) And not Woman liberated (the woman-female in her that no longer kills all female rivals, the woman-male in her that will no longer kill all males-rivals, woman's liberation of man, thus). But the Metaphysical Woman—the Secret Woman: this most concealed word in the concealed Jewish language-game: the *Shekhinah*.

To her is dedicated what follows, to the end.

2

Shekhinah, or the Road of Purity

The quality of mercy is not strain'd
It droppeth as the gentle rain from heaven . . .

Though justice be thy plea, consider this,
That in the course of justice, none of us
Should see salvation: we do pray for mercy.

. . . LET'S GO OUT FOR A LONG WALK, my beloved. It is good and clear outside. The serpent is asleep in the cage and the black raven is asleep also. I conjure space, and the tame distances are coiled around my chest: how calm and ample is the distant Ganges and how close the lullaby the dark-haired woman sings in her tiny bark—the slow-paced song, so familiar and so good to them, the distant tan-skinned men and women, so new and unfamiliar to us. See how good and clear everything still is. The song and the space—of space and time—unfold now. The song starts where it is first heard and so it continues: as the churning of the Ocean. Vishnu, the preserver and saviour of Brahma's ever renewed cosmic creation, rests asleep upon the liquid Deep, the thousand-headed snake Sesa (the Remainer—Ananta the Endless) of the quiet primeval Ocean supporting him.

How ample, serene and decided is everything! And so is the Evil One within the Deep, the Awakened One. Who acts: the liquid Deep, unquiet now, is by his will about to overtake, flood and destroy all Creation.

Vishnu, awakened by it, descends. He, the great Tortoise now, Kūrma, of the bottom. On his back he placed cosmic Mount Mandara and ordered the great Serpent to turn the mountain in the manner of an Indian peasant churning the butter, as if around the churning rod of a milk vessel, and to twirl it. The churning motion of the Serpent, of Vishnu himself, started, one end of the snake being pulled by the forces of good, the army of Devas, the other end by good's *half-brothers*, the army of Asūras, the forces of evil. Good and evil together helped Vishnu to rescue Creation. Vishnu the Tortoise, the Mount and the Snake now, as he has been and becomes Fish and Boar, the Man-Rama and Krishna. As he was Varūna Vasudeva in his Indo-European formation, when the Vedic "male"-dominated world came to India and overtook the female-male (the Secret Woman)-dominated world of pre-Vedic—Harappān—India.

And slowly, slowly the pre-Vedic sentiment of growth-in-earth, growth-in-water and in clouds, the plant-and-serpent wet sentiment (the tree forces, later yakshā, yakshi; the water forces, later nagā, nagi-ni; Śiva-Śakti of mature Hinduism; Adi-Buddha-Prajñāpāramitā of latest Buddhism), slowly the sentiment of sensuous plenitude, of continuum, and "moon's" nocturnal splendour overtook and then espoused the "masculine" conquering universe of "sunny" precision, of concrete divisive and delimiting abstracting, of discontinuity and then of harmonization, introduced by the trans-Himalayan nomadic and semi-nomadic warrior-invaders and their sacrifice-and-word worshipping priesthood: the Vedic-Aryan invaders of the pre-Vedic, Harappān, second millennium B.C. culture.

Slowly, very slowly the symbiosis of the two worlds gave what India became: the abstract-discontinuous-harmonizing world of the Rig-Vedas and Brahmanas; then the plenitude-continuum of the Upanishads (ātman-Brahman self-Self); in Buddhism, the enlightened abstracting-discontinuous-harmonizing world of the early and "pure" Buddhism, with its ideal of *arhat*, the "worthy" one who alone achieved Bliss; and the fullness—touch, smell, sound, word, one multi-oneness —of Buddhism's Great Vehicle and its Bodhisattva ideal.

(And isn't it true that the way great human historical collectives or tiny human—creative—individuals com-pose their productive and distributive deeds, their exchanges and changes—their life—is the

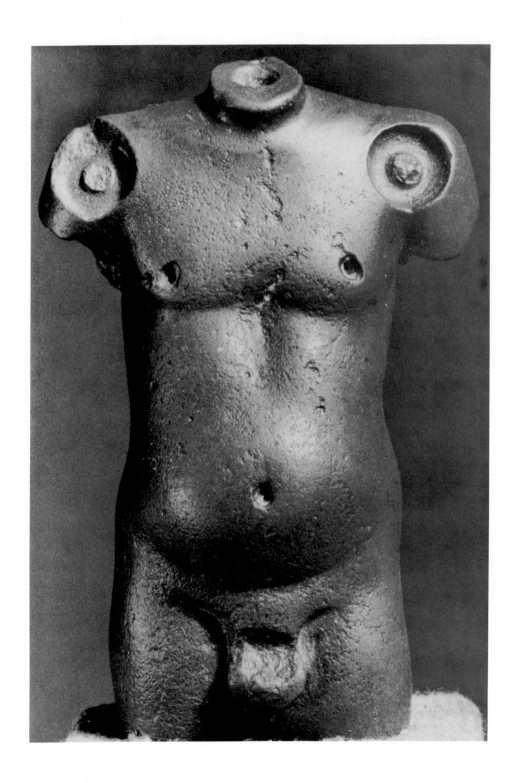

6. *Red sandstone torso from Harappā.*

7. *Portrait statue of Kaniṣka.*

8. *Buddha head, from Haḍḍa, Afghanistan.*

9. *Head of a Buddha, Mathura style.*

10. *"Court Scene" from Amarāvatī.*

11. *Buddha Preaching the First Sermon in the Deer Park at Varanasi.* Found at Sarnath.

12. *The Bodhisattva Avalokiteśvara-Padmapāni* (detail). Ajanta, Cave I.

13. *Ravana Shaking Mount Kailash.* Kailashanath complex, Ellora.

14. *Durga, the Slayer of the Titan Buffalo.* From Mamalapuram.

15. *Śiva Natarāja.* South India.

16. *Śiva Ardhanārī*. Śiva temple, Elephanta cave.

very way they com-pose their way of seeing, hearing, touching, creating things—their art? Pre-Vedic India of the Woman com-posed and gave fleshy plenitude, plastic fluidity, consistency and motion to its sculpted male figure (*Plate 6*); later, in the second "barbarian" invasion, the Śaka-Kushāna [*ca.* the first to third century A.D.] of Asia's northern steppes gave to India the restless, acute, dramatic, thus "mobile" rigidity of their sculpted warrior-chiefs (*Plate 7*); the braiding of both, now the one now the other accented, later gave India the rigidly geometrized contours of Gandhara's sensuous Helleno-Roman Buddhist icons (*Plate 8*) [Gandhara art: not, as it is usually considered, a late and provincial Roman art's imitation only], gave to Mathurā's sensuous fleshiness [legacy of Harappā] the dramatic rigidity of the Northern steppe humanity (*Plate 9*); hence the art of Amarāvatī (*Plate 10*); that of the Gupta era (*Plate 11*) and of the Cāḷukya and Pallava (*Plates 12, 13, 14*).)

In the great myth of India, the churning of the primeval milky Ocean, all the most precious things and beings of existence were about to be submerged and lost in the evil-lorded Deluge. And Vishnu descended into the Deep to rescue Brahma-the-Creator's world, he, now the Pillar-Mountain, the Great Serpent, as well as the Tortoise, of the churning miracle. He descended there not as the "male" Varūna-Vishnu, the preserver of stability, of cosmic order and human universal law (*ṛta*), but as the preserver and saviour of all metamorphoses, of all plenitude-changes (in a flash of solidarity-vision: the *chatoyant* silks of Iranian medieval weavers, now green, now red, blue, purple, gold, blue, as light and penumbra would have it!); not only as Vishnu's solar saviour-avatars, Fish, Tortoise, Boar, Lion-man, Dwarf, then Rama, then Krishna finally, almost, but as Vishnu's "lunar" radiations and adhesions, Vishnu-Brahmā-Śiva, the three-one, Trīmurti; He, also Śiva-Krishna, the multiple-present Dancer (Natarāja) (*Plate 15*) made one with his same and his "else," the He-She, lingam-yoni, his spouse, the Padmā (Lotus) Lakśmī, Śiva's beautiful Pārvatī, his heroic Durgā, his devouring Kāli, the Woman, the multiple Oneness, plenitude, continuum, the Woman-*via*-Man, the Man-*via*-Woman (*Plate 16*).

One of the last of treasures, Lakśmī herself, emerged from the churned Ocean, rescued with Vishnu's help and the help of the primeval half-brothers, the *devas* of the world of the Good, the *asuras* of the world of Evil acting together—this most subtle legacy of India.

Thus was Creation saved, by the presence and the power of metamorphoses:

Power equated with total plenitude, total continuum-interlace, I-with-in-cosmos. Yoga: power acquired more and more by diminishing more and more what is discontinuous in it, the separated ego and the separated, discontinuous senses around and in it. Thus India never knew or practiced asceticism in the West's Judaeo-Christian sense of the co-sufferer's redeeming-sacrificial compassion, but only in the sense of I-with-in-cosmos's com-passion, in the *prajnā-karuna* (wisdom-compassion) equation's sense, the matter-of-factness of knowing that everybody and everything co-exists in both destruction, thus self-and-else's destruction, and salvation, thus self-and-else's salvation.[1] Śiva-Śakti Embrace. Yoga. Yoga of History.

India:

Slowly, slowly, through many centuries, the funnel-like ample northern opening of India's expanse—the Indus-Ganges basin—was letting the dual Indian current flow, trickle down the walls of the ever narrowing cone—the immense Deccan and its extreme opposite southern opening, the Tamil area. When this descent—trickling—of Indian substance had reached the narrow funnel issue, its very intensity —Tamil's Vedantic, Vaiṣṇavite and Śaivite ardours—provoked within the funnel a backward and upward surge of the same substance, now immensely intensified, reaching again the Himalayan threshold, absorbing there, integrating the ripe Buddhism: Śiva-Vishnu's metamorphosis made one with the metamorphoses of Buddhism. India's creation— *chatoyant* silks!—The Bodhisattva Avalokiteśvara (the forever-to-be Buddha) Padmapāni (She-He Lotus-in-hand) made one same-else with the Supreme Buddha Amitābha of the Body of Bliss (Sambhogakāya), one with Vishnu and one with the Beloved: Vishnu Krishna, Krishna finally! *Not* Krishna the "male" teacher and counselor in the most ethical text of India, the Bhagavad Gitā, the counselor of his friend, the Pandava Arjuna, and the appeaser of his humane scruples at the start of the great fratricidal battle of Kurukshetra, but Krishna, the beloved Youth of the *Gita Govinda* songs-poems;[2] the lover of the gōpi Radha, the lover "grieved at separation," lunar lover of all gōpis, and lover of all men, young and old, of children, of springs, of summers, rivers, clouds, cows, of grass and mountains.

And Krishna Govinda, Krishna—the poetry, the music, the dance and the hope of India!—was all that remained. For Krishna *is* Avalokiteśvara! Krishna the same-else. And this is why Buddhism left India for elsewhere. And this is why it is in my song. In the song only.

And the song remains and continues. The dark clouds high in the sky now gather menacing, the monsoon. But here and in Krishna's embrace, all is blissful still. The late spring. Let's go for a long walk, my beloved. It is good and clear outside. The serpent is asleep in the cage and the black raven is asleep also. I conjure space and all the tame distances are coiled around my chest. How calm and ample is the distant river; how close and sweet the lullaby, the slow-paced song the young woman in the narrow bark is singing!

The song and the space—of space and of time—unfold now (*Plate 17*). The song starts where it is first heard and so it continues. As the poet's confession:

That the sameness of all distances is the very "else," the poignant else in the heart of what is poetry. The farthest far away in me, say, the unperceivable blinding moment-thought of my own death (impossible! "To be or not to be." That is the question posed a-fresh), and the close brutal awareness of my "abstract," thus lying sympathy with the agony of all and each of the men, women and children dying in a bombarded, far away open city; and, still closer, the closest to both bliss and futility, that trembling beauty of a dark, luscious winter rose, trembling on its long stem one rainy day against the wall of Granada's Isabellan Royal Chapel, in distant Spain—this is all one contemporary event, a poignant, justified hug of same-else in the heart of some poetry, already written there!

The serpent is still asleep in his-her cage; the black raven is asleep also. Let's go for a longer walk, my beloved. The road is peace-exhaling across the undulating greeting welcome of Massachusett's fields. Let's sit and rest a while here on this low rock at the entrance of New England's perhaps loveliest and most "poignant" old one-store village, Granville, in front of the big seigneurial house there, my, wanderer's, choice: the early nineteenth-century brick house at the edge of the road's entry is beautiful.

Its beauty is the "poignant" beauty of revived Greek proportionality, the neo-Palladian classical "thatness" of its elements and their interrelations, the windows, doors, and the silhouette of the entire structure—revived in the midst of the turbulence, brutality, uncertainties, dangers and boldness (oh, the red, trembling red rose in far off Andalusia!) of that distant republican age of America. Poignant vision and momentum of a late New England spring! The dense, throbbing, tall rosebush just under that window to the right of the stepped en-

17. ARTHUR POLONSKY: *The Song and the Space.*

trance door! I saw the window closed and secret—secretly opened; I heard the gentle noise of the window's sudden opening and perceived a lovely young girl's figure gently bending over the window sill to reach the scent of the roses below. Zosia! Zosia, the graceful, beautiful and bold Polish heroine of Adam Mickiewicz's epic.[3] How radiant is her young face—the radiant bliss of her sixteenth birthday this very fragrant, sunny morning. "Oh whatta beautiful mor–ning!" Love, happiness aureole her golden head; insecurity, danger, boldness surround her on all sides, invisible and present-threatening. Such was the vision of the bard who in his two monuments of Polish epic and dramatic poetry, *Pan Tadeusz* and *Dziady*, had chanted the greatness and the misery, the misfortunes, the awakenings and the sins of his beloved father-mother land, the unhappy Poland-Lithuania of the early nineteenth century.

> *O Lithuania, my fatherland,*
> *Thou art like health;*
> *What praise thou shouldst command*
> *Only that man finds who has lost thee quite.*
> *Today I see, and limn, thy beauty bright*
> *In all its splendour, for I yearn for thee.*[4]

Zosia, the poet's lovely Lithuanian child of old, bending now over the window sill to reach the scent of a Lithuanian rose. Far far away—very close. It was the purity of the Massachusetts house (purity as loyalty to origins; here the perennial revival of the Hellenic legacy: that beauty, goodness and truth are one and the same, instantly, irreducibly, a legacy transferred into the idiom of architecture that was the "purity" of Zosia's home in Lithuania).

The same—the same-else—purity or loyalty to the origins of man's never tarnished, never exhausted or made banal nostalgia of lost paradise!

Let's go for a still longer walk, my beloved—along and down the road of purity—the long forgotten country roads where, in the thick of wild greenery, lordly, half-ruined abandoned homes could still be found, the *genteel* house in Granville, the rural mansion in Lithuania, and across the vastness of Russia, Poland and the Ukraine, the "pure" houses and mansions, "houses of gentility," and their inhabitants long dead, alive and innocent of all social sins in the touching, poignant poems and narratives of the romantic lore, Pushkin, Mickiewicz, Turgenev.

For the sameness of all distances—in time, space, relation—is the very else, the poignant else in the heart of what is poetry.

The poignant architecture-purity of the lovely mansions of haughty "goyim" is the same-else purity, in quantity, in quality, in substance, of this Volynian humble *shtieble*.[5]

Let's stop, and enter there where the light expects us.

The Hassidic interior is poor and clean-washed. The candlelight and the white table cloth tell the truth of the Sabbath meal's solemnity. The third ritual meal is finished. The men seated at the table listen enraptured. The Rabbi speaks. Nobody interrupts. Nobody ever interrupts.

"The moment you think you are ready to know who is good and who is evil, that very moment you are not ready to know what is the good and what is the evil in life. For it is the moment of your pride and not the moment of your truth.

"And this is what my great-grandfather, Baal Shem Tov,[6] blessed be his name, meant when on his deathbed he said the words of the Psalmist 'Let not the foot of pride overtake me.' And this is the meaning of our prophet Jeremiah's 'God is in things farther from him . . .'"[7]

Rabbi Nachman of Bratislaw[8] remained silent. A sweet low singing and praying of the assembled men filled the darkened room.

The great-grandchild of the Besht continued: "A friend told me once: 'I dislike people busy with Justice. I like people with whom Justice is busy, I dislike people busy, busy with Justice.' For spirit—what justice is—is the difficult. It is easier—nearer to satisfaction—for a man plunged in meditation on the mysteries of the Torah to speak about the great mysteries of divine creation and divine revelation than about the little domestic, family and marketplace worries, obsessions and necessities. It is more spiritual to be with the mysteries of the body (everyday bread) than with the mysteries of the spirit (everyday's study of God's Law). This is what the Maggid of Meseritz, the learned Rabbi Dov Baer,[9] meant when he said 'Baal Shem taught me the language of the birds and the trees.'

"It is not a 'goyish' foolishness, or, still worse, a treason to the sacredness and exclusiveness of the study of the Law, to love the song of birds in the morning summer light or this light itself; the joy of the eye, the joy of the dancing, of the singing."

Rabbi Nachman, the rebel zaddik,[10] remained silent again for a while.

And then: "Connections connected. Connected. Everything is connected and I cannot see the end of it. I cannot see the beginning of it. Yet, the saying itself that there is no end and no beginning is already the measuring it with its own measure of a beginning and an end. Reality is this. Mystery is this. Continued, discontinued. And the zaddik knows it. That is what I heard one of them say once: 'There are miracles under my chair, but I do not want to bend down and pick them up.'[11] And no more about miracles. Miracles under the Hassid's bench.

"Would this be the real meaning of what rabbis and poets have said about real humility? That 'the spirit of God rests upon the head of the humble'? And what is it to be humble and yet proud of the search? —asks the zaddik. I, the real, the only zaddik,[12] am the same as the child I was, when spending hours at the tomb of my great-grandfather, away from the studious and stuffy beth ha-midrash,[13] I begged him to reveal to me the secret of his own humility. For I had already read what the most secret of all *Mishnas,*[14] *The Book of Splendor* or of Radiance,[15] had to reveal:

'. . . It is the souls of the righteous, *they alone,* which effect the true devotion of the Community of Israel to God, and her longing for him, for *these souls make possible the flow of the lower waters toward the upper* [italics mine], and this brings about perfect friendship and the yearning for mutual embrace in order to bring forth fruit.'[16]

"And 'from below must come the impulse to move the power above.'[17] And: 'Have we not heard it said that a serving maid at the Red Sea was vouchsafed greater vision than Ezekiel?'"[18]

[*Aside*: Isn't this to be identified with India's equation *samsara* = *nirvana,* the transient=permanent? Or with the Judaeo-Christian secret and similar aspiration, hopes and directions? Yes, of course. No— not exactly. The people of the Ten Commandments, when they are *loyal to their origins*, are loyal also to humility's so Judaic and so proud identity: Talmud's "where there is the Book, there is no Sword." For man is born with the love to kill. It takes a great humility to give up this price-full and praise-full love for the price-less and praise-less *amor intellectualis dei.*].

Another moment of meditation and melodious silence followed.
"Such is the meaning of our *debekuk*, of our clinging to God: the meaning of Torah's—the Book's—Law, and of the purity of intention (*kavannah*) in following the Law in each of our everyday actions—and not elsewhere. And here is, here should be, the joy of the Hassid. For joy—the pleasure in our body—is unseizable; the measure, the total measure of pleasure is the very measure of our total body, outer and inner. There is no room there left, no void left where mind's perception or vision could penetrate.

"Pleasure is unseizable: the unseizable, hidden *Eyn-Sof*—no-end, infinity; it is *Ayin*: the nothing.[19] Only pain is seizable. Total pleasure is seized—revealed—when localized: as pain. Pain is localized pleasure. Sex. Ecstasy. Dance. That is why and how we dance and pray. 'Serve the Lord with gladness; come before His presence with singing' (Ps. 100:2). In festive white robes. On the last evening of the yearly feast of Torah's joy we men dance and sing, hugging the sacred and adorned scrolls to our breasts. We, praying and dancing mothers, hug the Torah as mothers hug their babes. Women we are men. But this is precisely what, for the great Rabbi Elijah ben Salomon, the Gaon of Vilna,[20] the greatest foe of our present Hassidism,[21] was abomination. It was what, for the prophet Elijah, was the worshiping of Baal.

"For him the unseizable, immeasurable infinity could be also seized, could be measured not even within the still unseizable mystery of revealed Torah itself, not even within the interpreted confines of the ritual that surrounded, fenced and protected the sacredness of that written and oral law, but, deeper-narrower, in the strict obedience to this revealing ritual itself. For him the unseizable totality was seized then in its precise humble fragment.

"The Hassidic hugging dance—the dance in the open, green, 'goyish' fields facing the sun, the stars, the storms and snow, the distant hills and the rapid waters, the Torah dance was abhorrent to him. A pagan foolishness. And pagan and 'goyish' it possibly was.[22] For the great Gaon knew the joy of substitution only: the finite for the infinite. We, Hassidim, we know also the joy of infinite correspondence, the same-else, the discontinued-continued: the hugging dance of the Law, the dance of the Child hugging against his heart and mind the humble grass seen, grown, betwixt the rain-washed cobblestones of his native *shtetle's*[23] street. The smiling, sunlit, stone-hugging street grass—

sparks of fresh green goodness uplifted by man's *mitzvah*,[24] child's heart and mind, out of their evil imprisonment, that's what, at the tomb of Baal Shem Tov, was given to me as my great-grandfather's own, childhood's, joy.

"And joy it was, the unseizable totality of pleasure (goodness) commensurable with my body only, created-seized in my body as pain (evil): the same-else, the discontinued-continued. The joy-pain of all the created worlds, created in three simultaneous stages.

"A three-one stage: the stage of the Grass, of child's illumination by touch, by sight; the stage that grew out from this child-heart's illumination, the stage of meditation, of permanence, of giving, of belonging, the new world of the ruminant Cow—my first encounter, my great-grandfather's first encounter, I was sure of it, in a forest stable, with a big cow's head, the frontal, sudden and very ancient (Abram's, Isaak's, Yacob's), emergence of a huge, calm, cliff-like and sexy thing— a mountain, not a being yet, not a muzzle either—very near, very imposing, yet very protecting, with, behind it, another thing of shining and absorbing friendliness, a new thing from beyond the slow glance of the ruminant's eyes. And forever after, in loyalty to this never again reconstructed origin and event, there was present to me the same child's —my great-grandfather's—presentiment that, beyond or beneath any object emerging sudden and very ancient and erotic, I might seize my certitude of infinity.[25]

"The certitude of *infinity*, the last, the third stage, the stage that grew with the Grass and out from the glance of the ruminant Cow, the stage of the Secret Woman. The plenitude, the return, the rebirth, the redemption *without-Redeemer*, the Woman.

"The world at once of the joy of the Torah and the three-one pleasure-pain of the soul: the soul-grass, soul body, the *nefesh*; the soul-cow, the soul-soul, *ruah*; the soul-woman, soul-spirit, *neshamah*, Shekhinah-Light."[26]

[*Aside*: all this soul-structure is what the Jewish painter Chaim Soutine[27] painted in his harmonies—his three-one plenitude—of distortion.]

"As the Book of Splendor says: 'We know that three souls pertain to the divine grades. Nay, four, for there is one supernal soul which is unperceivable, certainly to the keeper of the lower treasury, and even to that of the upper. This is the soul of all souls, incognizable and inscrutable. All is contingent on it, which is veiled in a dazzling bright veil.

From it are formed pearls which are tissued together like the joints of the body, and these it enters into, and through them manifests its energy. . . . Yet another, a female soul, is concealed amidst her hosts and has a body adhering to her through which she manifests her power, as the soul in the human body.

"'These souls are as copies of the hidden joints above. Yet another soul is there, namely, the souls of the righteous below, which, coming from the higher souls, the soul of the female and the soul of the male, are hence preeminent above all the heavenly hosts and camps. . . .'[28]

"Also: 'When is "one" said of a man? When he is male together with female and is highly sanctified and zealous for sanctification. . . .'"[29]

[*Aside*: Śiva-Śakti in their embrace-union? Śiva, the perennial, undisturbed—passive!—serenity-repose, Śakti, the perennial energy of endless creativity, in union-embrace?

No. But—through which underground, never blocked channels of Judaic influences on our West?—the Presence, as in this most open and daring imagery of Picasso's (*Plate 18*), here, the whole humanity graded—old grand woman, young woman-torero, little girl, big human monkey—watching, *witnessing* the great initial event of body-and-mind's judgment and mercy, simply—error or truth?—the great initial event of cosmic creation: a kneeling male unmasking himself, taking off the *mask* of aggressive bull, the mask of minotaur, and a young, graceful woman, hovering, nude, over him in a dancing tiptoe pose, pouring, ejecting into him—*picador* and *torero* at once—his own male seeds of pro-creation. She—Picasso's whole secret—the man-*via*-woman, the woman-*via*-man, supreme, supernal mother-father-daughter, Light, Light of the Presence, Shekhinah. (And who is it, dancing there—over six centuries ago!—in ceremonial attire, among grandees of Portugal's royal court and the flamboyant night-moving torches, along the streets of Alcobaça? Youthful Pedro I, the recently enthroned King of Portugal, the maddened revenger of his murdered Ines.

Ines de Castro, the young Castilian gentlewoman, Dom Pedro of Portugal, names of lovers never forgotten in Portugal's legend, history and sentiment: how they met and fell at once and madly in love, at that noisy state festivity of betrothal—of young Dom Pedro, son of the astute Alfonso IV, to the Infanta Constança of Castile, whose companion Ines was—poor, poor Infanta!—how then, at the first touch of their hands, the court dance demanding it, and the touch of their eyes —joy! surprise!—the destiny of their passion was sealed; how after the early, premature death of the young Constança [poor, poor Constança wounded unto death, her story still to be told], Dom Pedro and Doña Ines wedded clandestinely, how the happiness of their body-as-mind solidarity—the shared gentle harmony of their intertwined dispositions, their love of song and verse, of Coimbra's hills and the Montego's murmur at nightfall, away from the brutality of the age—was destroyed: the murder of Ines in Pedro's absence, ordered, for reasons of state security, by Alfonso IV and his councilors—the fury and the bloody rebellion of the prince against his father, and then, this finale

18 PABLO PICASSO: *La Danse des Banderilles.*

in Portugal's proudest and most congenial lore: Pedro's ascending the
throne and his ordering of Ines's cadaver to be transported in funerary
grandiose procession from Coimbra to the Court of Alcobaça, the tri-
umphal coronation at the Castle of Alcobaça of his now legitimate
Queen, her terrifying cadaver, wrapped in royal splendor, given at the
King's order the ceremonial hand-kissing homage by all the assembled
grandees of the realm, and the murderers of Ines de Castro caught and
executed. It was that very night that Pedro I was dancing in the streets
of Alcobaça, the grandees, the torches, the people witnessing in awe the
sensuous and solemn, severe and poignant dance of Iberian and Moorish
curve. A dance of revenge, the complete measure of revenge having
been reached. Indeed.

Yet why were there tears on the dancer's face? Here: his dance
was the dance, the very dance Ines de Castro danced at their first encounter there at the feast of the betrothal. Lovely Ines danced then—
how admired by all!—the sensuous and solemn, severe and poignant
dance of Iberian-Moorish curve. And now the dance of Ines was Dom
Pedro's. Dom Pedro *via* Ines, Ines *via* Pedro, the woman-*via*-man, the
man-*via*-woman. The Light of the Presence. Shekhinah.]]

"And Zohar continues: 'It behooves a man to be "male and female," always, so that his faith may remain stable, and in order that the
Presence may never leave him. You will ask: How with the man who
makes a journey, and, away from his wife, ceases to be "male and
female"? Such a one, before starting, and while he still is "male and
female" must pray to God, to draw unto himself the Presence of his
Master. After he has prayed and offered thanksgiving, and when the
Presence is resting on him, then he may go, for by virtue of his union
with the Presence he is now male and female in the country, just as he
was male and female in the town. . . .

"'Moreover, it is his duty, once back home, to give his wife
pleasure, inasmuch as she it was who obtained for him the heavenly
union.'[30]

"'. . . she it was who obtained for him the heavenly union.'

"This is what my great-grandfather Baal Shem told his future
wife at their first secret meeting, this and other things hidden from the
majority of people, high and low. But he knew then at once that Hannah would accept him and his vision-thought as he wished it. And Hannah saw in his eyes, perceived in the sound of his voice, the presence of

a very ancient, very majestic ancestral feeling—the presence of Tenderness.

"She saw Tenderness: she saw the poignant solitude of man, of the world, of the mind, and she saw the poignant solidarity of man, of the world and of the mind united, made one in origin, one in scope, never separated from each other. She saw the Secret Woman thus present at the creation *ex nihilo*: of man, of the world, of the mind. And it was the poignant Tenderness.

"And Hannah, my great-grandmother, blessed be her name and her memory, the first Hassida, became Baal Shem's untiring, most loyal companion and sharer till her last day on earth.

"Tenderness: Solitude-Solidarity: Shekhinah."

The Rebbe Nachman of Bratislaw spoke no more. The assembly, dismissed, dispersed into the peaceful darkness of a Sabbath evening. How far far away in meaning, in usage, was all this and the *shtieble*! How near, very near around my chest all distances were coiled together! The *shtieble* where the "pure" Hassid was presiding, was at the end of my road of origins and of loyalty, the road of purity. And so the end was also the beginning of another—the *same*—road, the road of *meditation*.

3
The Road of Meditation

Paul Klee on the spiral:

Changing length of the radius, combined with peripheral motion, transforms the circle [Klee's "purest of mobile forms"] into the spiral. Lengthening of the radius creates a vibrant spiral. Shortening of the radius narrows the curve more and more till the lovely *spectacle dies suddenly in the static center. Motion here is no longer finite, and the question of direction regains new importance. This direction determines either a gradual liberation from the center through freer and freer motions or an increasing dependence on an eventually* destructive *center. [Emphasis mine.]*

This is the question of life and death. . . .[1]

*   *   *

I. So be it:

The Secret Woman—the Shekhinah—is the most mysterious image-word in Judaism, fascinating to, yet avoided, even feared by, Halakhic[2] rabbinical thought, exalted and lordly in what is called Jewish mysticism, the Kabbalah—the two worlds never blended together, always together; the world of the secret and sovereign male, the world of the sovereign, secret woman.

Shekhinah—image-abstraction, image without attributes, never image-icon, image-body—image nevertheless—*chatoyant* silk! pure abstraction (pure: loyal to its ontological origins) and "pure" image (pure: loyal to its cognitive origins). For the concept of Incarnation is the most repulsed—most repulsive—concept in "pure" Judaism (pure, that is, in its psycho-historical origins). Hence the mystery, the fascination and the power of its creative—hidden historical—impact. When after centuries of integrative growth—from the Merkabah[3] abstracted imagery and the gnostic, later neo-platonic apports, to the moral-pietist severity of the eleventh-twelfth century Italo-German Hasidei Ashkenaz[4]—the Kabbalah fully asserted itself, first in tormented "heretic" (Catharist) twelfth-century Provence, then in adjacent and kindred Catalonia, would it not be the presence-impact there of the hidden, the Secret, Woman as purest Judaic abstraction, and as purest Christianized image-Incarnation, the Virgin Mary, that brought to fruition the centred image-and-concept of the lovable and lovely sovereign Lady in the West's twelfth-century poetic-philosophical invention, the poetry of that age and that chivalry, the poetry of the *trovar clus*?

But the main thing here, at the start of the road of meditation, remains the same as when the road was still the road of purity, or of origins and of loyalty (and where my mysterious companion, the beloved, remained and so I remain now and here alone): the Secret Woman remains the most mysterious and central image-word in Judaism. For the mystery of and in this word is still the same mystery the young, orphaned Baal Shem revealed—so his great-grandchild Rabbi Nachman of Bratislaw of the "pure" *shtieble* learned and revealed—to his Hannah; the same intimate mystery Baal Shem unveiled to his two most faithful and cherished disciples, the Maggid of Meseritz and Jacob Joseph of Polona[5] who, each separately, changed at the contact of his Shekhinah-thought from the élitist, haughty "male" animosity of Halakhic scholars into a devotional loyalty to his healing message—the Hassidic "lifting of the spark" of the good, hidden and found purposefully through the poignancy of the Grass, the Cow, the Woman, in the very darkness of Evil's shards—and thus became the intellectual co-founders of his new Hassidism.

From Kabbalah's renewed, *uso populo*, ancient creed, the "descent on behalf of the ascent," from the renewed ardour of messianic passion and universal hope reawakened by the seventeenth-century's bloody tragedy of the Chmielnicki holocaust and the Shabbatean messianic failure of this hope—a hope so lasting and yet so creative—from all this the new Hassidism was born with Baal Shem as the healing, saving-without-saviour, purely Jewish moral-pietist creed of salvation *via* correction. A healing creed in its in-depth purpose, it was also, in its in-depth result, the self-liberating creed.

Was not the Judaic passion for the concealed meaning—the *abstracted* image-expression—in any thing and any being (hence the Judaic repulsion for any *incarnating* art=idolatry), was not this passion accepted, and was not its irrepressible creative urge transferred entirely into the exclusive art of image-concept, the exalted art of image-word, the art of metaphor bearing poetry, the verbal imagery of the Haggadic-Midrashic[6] and, rooted there, Kabbalah's verbal inventions?

But was it not from within the world of the Hassidic or Hassidic-inspired *shtetle*, the dense, narrow, deep and humble world of precisely this most exalted Jewish passion for the image-metaphor, that a great cultural change came?

It came of course along channels of slow social-cultural awakening: the ghetto's and ex-ghetto's self-liberation came when, subtly infiltrating there from the "goyish" outside, from the West's, the greater West's nineteenth and twentieth centuries' own self-liberation, the dignity of *techne*, the dignity of man's thinking *via* body's "ten-fingered grasp of reality"[7] *via* the image-touch, rose up from its subservience to the oppressing priority of *Sophia*, the sovereignty of thinking in image-concepts. It is then that as a proving, revealing symbol of an age of planetary revolution, the Jewish self-liberation of the "pure" image-touch, image-body, took place, the equalization of its dignity with that of the "pure" image-concept; for the first time in the history of that people and their culture, the visual-manual arts—the creation of the touch-smell-taste-vision-pose-abstraction in painting, sculpting, dancing—and their equalization with "purely" speculative and scientific thought, were now exuberantly achieved.

Kabbalah's doctrine of the mystery of "the descent on behalf of the ascent" *via* the Presence—the Shekhinah—the Light, the Secret, Metaphysical Woman, a doctrine made one with Kabbalah's still more mysterious doctrine of the cosmic initial Error caused by the severity and rigor of "pure" Father-judgment, the Error corrected-redeemed by the "fiat" of the Secret Woman's Mother-mercy—this is what in in-depth expression and in in-depth diffusion the *shtetle* gave us.

The sixteenth-century West's (secretly Kabbalah-oriented) passionate belief in the concreteness, the *fleshiness* of abstraction was revived in the twentieth-century West's crypto-kabbalist visual-manual thought, the thought and art of a Picasso, a Miró, a Paul Klee: that cosmos equated with mind is "pure" creation, creation loyal to its origin of being the new, the unexpected, the first, thus the "monstrous," thus without respectability in it, with only respect and the serious in it, a thing-"monster," comical, distorted. This thought and this art were joined by the thought and art that equated soul with male-and-female, with judgment-and-mercy, with the moral imperative without limitations, the thought and art of Jewish twentieth-century soul-laborers, Chaim Soutine, Max Weber, Levine, Ben Shahn, Chagall, Lipchitz, Epstein and so many others who came and are still coming in this sudden flowering.

*   *   *

Is then the mysterious itself waning away with its mystery's historico-dialectical communication? Or does it remain as the very why of this communication itself, as the mystery of *unexpected* connections there? For, what is the connection between the meditative gravity, the tradition-centred majesty of the "pure" concept of Shekhinah, and, when set in *direct confrontation* with this concept, the "frivolity" of the concept of, say, visual arts? How to connect the image-word, Shekhinah, with, say, Degas' *le beau* [meaning, surely, in painting] *est un mystère*? Or with the *chatoyant* mysterious magic of Dosso Dossi?

What is meant by the word (=word-game), the mysterious, itself? Does it mean—at least here and now—"pure" meditation, that dimension of thought along which the thought reaches beyond the separating limits of what could be defined as labour of thought and as leisure of thought? Meditation: when and where speculative thought or *interrogation about reality is made one with reality itself.* When and where the interrogation "what is death and what is life, death-*via*-life, life-*via*-death? what is finity's (being's) possibility, non-finity (non-being's) impossibility temporally? is *aeternitas* the mind, is duration body or mind? what is the present and not-present, what is the particular and what is the general, the good and the evil?" (but never what is the true and the not-true there)—when and where the interrogation, the delight of speculation about reality is made one with reality itself—with life and death, true and not-true, duty and right.

Would it mean what it meant to that man who, desirous to learn as closely as possible the existential "secret" of a living fish, after having caught one from the deep, holding it tight in his closed hand, close to his eye, the poor fish fighting in his hand for its existence, turning convulsively and so rapidly between the encircling fingers of its captor that his observing eye could not follow and register either the char-

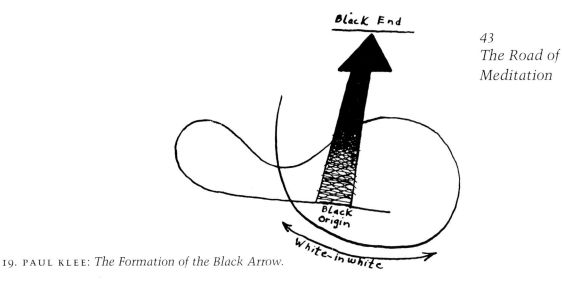

19. PAUL KLEE: *The Formation of the Black Arrow.*

acter of the motion or the changing aspect of the creature, saw that
finally one alternative remained; either to squeeze the palpitating fish
to death—and then to study it at ease, but as a dead thing only—a dead
study too; or to free it and let the living fish join its own living liquid
world. So he did. And plunging himself into the deep he continued,
deep-diver-like, his "objective" study, a study not one with his body
any more. Renouncing thus his earlier hopeless and erroneous goal.
Mysteriously *now* hopeless and *mysteriously* also erroneous. Was not,
aeons ago, the man a fish himself?

The mysterious would be and would remain not so mysterious:
it would be the *memory* of the fish in the man.

Bergson's *matière et mémoire*: the Creation *ex nihilo*, the Shekhinah in Kabbalah, is, in depth, the "pure" memory and matter of the
creation *ex nihilo*, the creation of the "black arrow" in Paul Klee (Plate
19). The same-else.

As the zaddik-"helper," Rabbi Shneur Zalman[8] said: "There are
miracles under my chair, but I do not want to bend down."

*   *   *

The same-else: the anger-bound man's meditation-answer and the
peace-bound man's meditation-question.

Angry man's first beating against the bars of his natal prison—
Piranesi's no-exit *Carceri* (*Plate 20*)—his response to the eye's escape
up there into the beyond-bars blue, the infinite white-clouded blue of
Tiepolo's sky.

a) *Angry man:*
"This finity-infinity, this being-no-being voluptuous ego

worries' 'language game,' let it remain with the *leisure* man, where it belongs. What has it to do with the *labour* man's worries—my worries of naked every-day existence?"

a₁) *The same-another-angry man:*

"*Soit.* The poor old Navaho woman sitting in her village marketplace among her earthenware pots to sell and waiting anxiously, desperately, to sell them—will there still be buyers this afternoon?— what has she to do with the voluptuous metaphysical anxiety of the infinity-thought? And yet: the Navaho old poor woman's entire and obscure opaque *is*ness, would it not be (at that moment of co-extension with her true existing) her entire, exactly total, thus certainly to herself and to others unseizable, anxiety? And is not therefore this very totality of the Navaho old woman's *is*ness-anxiety, obscure, opaque,

20. PIRANESI: From his *Carceri.*

unseizable, a substitution for, as well as a correspondence to what in our 'language-game' we call infinity? And would it not be, as a possible model, the real 'root of the roots' of any existence on any level: substitution-correspondence, solitude-solidarity, made one as Tenderness, as Rabbi Nachman had said?"

a₂) *Same-angry-another-other man:*

"True issue, Tiepolo's escape? *Soit.* A particular, individual *possibility.*"

(Peace-bound man's meditation-question, man's speculative thought-question about reality [what is death-*via*-life, life-*via*-death, finity, beginning, end; infinity, no-beginning, no end?]—and reality itself [the reality of good *versus* evil, of truth *versus* lie, of life-*versus*-death] making one.)

b) *Peace-bound man:*

"Lazy meditation all this, this basically metaphysical *a priori* crap, as a young convinced physicist of today would have it here? Yet, is it not also accepted today (philosophy, science, poetry not being 'ashamed' or afraid of confusion resulting from the danger of their mutual proximity), that, say, the *speculatively*, mathematically, posited, then scientifically, experimentally, confirmed, fact-event of a dying star's 'infinite density and zero volume'—a black hole—that this 'concrete' fact, unseizable in its totality as fact and even as concept could be described by a scientifically trained analyst as relying 'on mathematics and *in a sense on poetry*'? [9]

"Or today's astrophysical vision of an *ultimate* galaxy, beyond which no astrophysical space could exist or be; an ultimate galaxy in a universe with no ultimate in it; a vertigo-giving vision of an absolute limitation—an 'absolute' discontinuity—no-thing—in an 'unlimited' relativist space-time *continuum*? A plenitude-nothingness, plenitude-void—*sunyata*?"

b₁) *The same-another-other man:*

"*Soit.* A probability speculation about speculation and reality made one."

*   *   *

The quiet road of meditation's quest has many detours, each with its own obstacle-query, unquiet and unavoidable: "Loyalty to origins"—to what origins? The word "mystery," what does it mean beyond the mystery's word mystery being nothing else but mystery, "rose is a rose is a rose is a rose?" What is an image-touch, what is an image-concept *each being within the other*? What is then meant, again, here, by the same-else? Are those queries real obstacles?

Or aren't they any meditation's very "structure of behaviour"? The structure of vagueness itself, *of the idea of vagueness and not of what is vague, of a thing that is vague*? For does not vagueness mean—in its causation and effect—fusion, co-fusion, and not confusion? To be vague is indeed, in its cause, to be confused or to confuse the elements of thought. To be vagueness, in its cause and its effect, is to fuse, to be the fusion, the co-fusion of all the elements of thought. Each would be the structure and the content of thought. All of them are fused together in one *instantaneity*, the *immediacy* of thought's both *cumulative* and *one-pointed*, centred, moment. (Such the creation of a young woman's head in a drawing by Picasso (*Plate 21*), the two short, parallel and incurved initial lines of the neck growing—grown already—into the same-else curvatures of the entire head. Here is Picasso's typical prowess of instantaneity in endless-growth-final-achievement, with this artist's free chosen emphasis on the moment of growth, in contrast to, say, the typical Matisseian emphasis on the momentum of achievement (*Plate 22*); in both, nevertheless [and this is the very essence of any art], the simultaneity of culminative growth and of achievement being boldly given. Such the structure and content of any thought *ab initio*, of any knowledge *ab initio*, thus ultimately of any perception's freshness and *novelty*, the astonishing, thus unpredicted, novelty, the "monster," in any creative act of existence.

⋆　　⋆　　⋆

All this: plenitude-vagueness of co-fusion, the immediacy of equated, simultaneous genesis-process growth-achievement, all this is also, and emphatically so, the Jewish Kabbalah.

Avodak be-Gashmiyar—worship through corporeality—such was Baal Shem's message of persistent, *pleinière* joy-surprise, body's joy-the-first (Child's first discovery of Eros: the Eros of the street grass, of the cow, of the woman), never joy-the-second, joy without-surprise). This Hassidic revived message of classical Kabbalah is a *dual* message, at once generous, profit-less soul=cosmos's "descent on behalf of the ascent," and, in dialectic's *coincidentia contradictorum*, Kabbalah's profit-pointed magic constructs.

And who in his or her sober mind would accept today, besides

21. PABLO PICASSO: *Girl Having Her Hair Combed.*

22. HENRI MATISSE: *Seated Nude.*

some tired shelter-seeking "desperado" of the left-over anxiety-ridden aristocratic world, or the world of "bourgeois" anti-bourgeois daring disillusionment (its pseudo-Yoga, pseudo-Kabbalah lures), who would accept seriously and critically—and not rather reject with repulsion and even fear—Kabbalah's numerological-alphabetical semantics, its psycho-astrological calculi, the "mysterious" participation of letters-numbers-lights in the creation of the cosmos and man and of their destinies?

And yet . . .

And yet, who would not today be puzzled and challenged when confronted with the historical fact that during the so-called pre- and proto-scientific eras men and women of great mental and moral integrity could seriously and critically participate in the world of the speculative—as well as, sometimes, practical—"science" of magic: some great Light-theologians of the Christian medieval West and East, the Islamic Sufis, and the sophisticated kabbalists, the luminaries of Jewish meditation in thirteenth-century Gerona or Toledo, in sixteenth-century Safed or eighteenth-century Lithuania, and that this world was respected and studied even by austere, rationalist rabbis like the Gaon of Vilna?

Indeed, what made them, the learned leaders of Jewish "mystical" meditation, accept, wittingly, willingly, the vision of Vagueness-Plenitude as the very structure of Being, a vision so "vague" as frame-synthesis, and so precise and detailed as content-analysis? For such is Kabbalah's psycho-cosmic vision of the Divine Being as being before= after, not-yet=already the Creator-Emanator of existence; the Divine Infinity, the No-End, *Eyn-Sof*, its absolute Nothingness—*Ayin*—concealed in the externalia of thought's logic, a concealed thing absurdly co-extensive with what has no extension, and simultaneously revealed, manifested—the same-else!—in the interiority or subjectivity of thought (the only possible "objective" method of proof Kabbalah ever accepted) as a no-thing thought, a body-thought, thus a thing: Kabbalah's vision of the Divine Corporeality.

This is Kabbalah's great absolute, *Eyn-Sof*, whose unseizable totality is totally transferred into (thus seized by) the act—the primeval first act? the primeval last one? the ever growing, never achieved, forever achieved, never growing, act of Infinity's self-contraction, the act of *zimzum*,[10] Infinity's self-reduction to the infinitesimal point-finity for whose corporeal finity of being (the *corpus simplicissimus* of Spinoza?) the Infinity of No-being, of Nothingness, is totally substituted.

This vision of substitution is the central and most daring doctrine of the later Lurianic Kabbalah[11] whose historical antecedent could already be found—so loyal is Kabbalah to its origins and its long tradition—in much earlier premises.

*   *   *

[*Aside*: In all that follows it is to be remembered that for me Kabbalah is the transfer of the world of medieval sacral cosmogonies into our world of profane epistemologies.]

Plethoric Vagueness: *Eyn-Sof*'s coming out within itself, Nothingness's self-manifestation as self-concealment (exactly the Spanish word *ensimismamiento*) and self-contraction—*zimzum*'s corporeality —is both an act of *absolute substitution and an act of correspondence with that that emanates in and from it*: the ten *Sefirot*-Emanations[12] (ten splendors of the Sapphire), their coming from=within, during= after=before Infinity's being the No-being, the Nothingness, the coming of the ten Powers (not attributes) of the Divine, the ten divine Creatures-Emanations all in each, each in the others, each in all at once, one Vagueness-Plenitude of instantaneity. And this coming out from the within and this remaining within the domain of the Divine, the domain of subjectivity, is what makes Kabbalah's *Sefirot*-Emanations so typically Judaic (they constitute the dynamic entirety of the Torah, the Law), so different from their historical prototypes, Neo-Platonic (the successive out-going Emanations of Plotinus) and even Gnostic (*aeons*).

The daring Lurianic doctrine of Creation—*Eyn-Sof*'s act of manifestation not as expansion, but as contraction-concealment, *zimzum* —of Creation's mysterious instantaneity of growth and achievement, contains the even more daring doctrine of the growth and achievement (as well as of the cause and effect) of the primeval Error—originally the Gnostic vision of a cosmogonic drama-catastrophe—the Error in the very act of creation to be corrected and redeemed.

And this Error is Adam Kadmon's, the Primeval Man's, the Ancient One's Error of not yet being male-and-female, male-*via*-female, female-*via*-male, still being judgment (*Din*) and mercy (*Rahamim*), and not judgment-*via*-mercy, mercy-*via*-judgment.

And then—simultaneously with this act of creation—the second act of creation *ex nihilo* unfolds:

When the *Light*, the Light of *zimzum* within-without its infinitesimal space—*tehiru*—and its "time that is no time" (as a Cordovero[13] would have it, the space-time of prayer, and of *mitzvah*)—when this Light, the ten *Sefirot*, manifested itself in the Light of Adam Kadmon's corporeality and when the Light's radiation and its weight became the very corporeality of its recipients—the vessels, *kelim*—then, under the pressure of the Light's weight, these vessels-*Sefirot* broke.

It is the psycho-cosmic drama of the *Breaking of the Vessels*.[14]

To the skin of the broken vessels' scattered shards, the matter, the flesh of Evil adhered. But also the flesh, the corporeality of the remaining Light, is to be found and released in them.

And the last, the tenth *Sefirah*, the farthest from, thus the closest also (in the universe of no distances and no dimensions) to the Source, the tenth *Sefirah*, *Malkhuth*, became the battleground of the struggle between the flesh of the Evil and the Good; the *Sefirah Malkhuth*, the abode of the Shekhinah, the abode of the all-*Sefirot*-containing Secret Woman.

The third and last act of the simultaneous drama starts and finishes here. It is Luria's vision of the Messianic correction of the Error and of its result, the Breaking of the Vessels: the vision of the *tikkun*, the Redemption of the primeval Error, not of the primeval Sin. For in the deepest and most intimate Jewish meditation, Adam's sin was the "impure" separation of one *Sefirah*-power from another, the sin of discontinuity and of interruption.

And the vision of Kabbalah is always of the descent on behalf of the ascent. The Redemption of the Error forever was, is, started, was, is, forever finished already in the very descent of each *Sefirah* into itself as concealed infinity (nothing-ness), as self-radiation, as self-reflection of creation's first act: Kabbalah's vision of the same-else, the vision of a dynamic continuum. The plenitude of the redeeming *tikkun* is already achieved in the very process-genesis of creation's act—the *zimzum*—the act of Substitution-and-Correspondence, and yet, at the very same time, this same plenitude is still to be achieved by the "purity," the "loyalty to the origins" of the creature-man, the "pure," the real, the only real Jew, by his loyalty to the Presence in him—the Presence in any righteous Jew, in any "loyal"—moral—man, of the Shekhinah.

*   *   *

This is what made them, the learned leaders of Jewish meditation,

accept the vision of Vagueness-Plenitude as the very structure of Being.

*   *   *

"No imagery satisfies me unless it is also knowledge."

Antonin Artaud

What are the "origins" in Kabbalah, what is the "loyalty" in the Kabbalah? Kabbalah's "purity"? Does Kabbalah differ from any other mystical meditations—and it does not: only in the degree of proximity to and distance from any meditation "loyal" to the Presence—the Secret Woman's Presence—say, in Tantric Buddhism, in medieval Christianity.

*   *   *

For Kabbalah is the hidden memory of the first spark man had seen—fear! surprise, joy!—and produced in the mutual touch, the rubbing, of two rock splinters. And the dimension of this memory—a sparkling memory-point—of a flame-to-be, of a light-to-be, grew up into the vertiginous dimensions of mind's and of cosmos's memory-sphere. It is what in the Zohar is called "the fleeting vision [of the Eternal], the beginning of the being"—*nathabet ha-yeshia*. Fleeting, evanescent is, indeed, the spark's being, the spark with-in the rock, the spark with-out the rock! And how could it come to be there? And so the great human query, human passion, *the passion of interiority*, man's equating his speculation about the real with the real itself, became the greatest, the acutest passion of Judaic query: not only the passion of the "beginning" —the spark! (*reshit*, this first word in the Bible)—but of what is within the rock, the before-the-beginning and the before the before-the-beginning. Hidden in the spark's identity, its substance—its destiny-to-be-ignition, to-be-light—is made one with the substance, the identity of the rock's interior, hidden, concealed within the concealment of the rock itself: the hidden spark is there not a thing-in-the-rock but a thing-in-the-mind, my mind. And there it is about to be the spark's corporeality, to be flesh: Antonin Artaud's "There is a mind in the flesh, a mind quick as lightning. . . ." The passion of interiority and the interiority itself are equated: the transfer from the abstract to the concrete is what at once activates there and validates the resulting inner-outer Vagueness of Plenitude—and the initial total tension inherent in it. For it is tension—in the interiority of the rock's mind, rock's belly, my belly—that, in Kabbalah's vision, originates the primeval coming out from concealment into the very same-else concealment and the creation then and there of the thing-to-be as a thing without end, without beginning, infinity itself—*Eyn-Sof*—as nothingness—*Ayin.* The no-being, nothingness, is and will be the in-being—the *spark, zimzum* and its destiny.

Vagueness-Plenitude. Tension in the primeval Will, as the majority of later kabbalists would have it? Tension in the primeval Thought, as the earlier kabbalists (Isaak the Blind in Provence, Azrael of Gerona) had thought? Or—for Kabbalah was never a dogma or a theology—as ibn Latif, the Spanish poet-kabbalist of the early thirteenth century saw it, will and thought joined together, in poet's prayer, "like a kiss"?

And this is how Kabbalah's vision of genesis-process, of process-achievement unfolds itself: it unfolds itself as a further expansion of the primeval transfer, the transfer from the rock's unseizable, uncorporeal pre-being, pre-spark, hidden in the bowels of the rock, its about-to-be-being—the spark—into the bowels of the mind, my mind. And this initial transfer from the "silence and secrecy" of the rock to the "discourse" of the mind, itself expands as the great transfer from mind's speculative onto-*cosmogonic*, onto-*cosmological* worries—what is the "beginning" of the universe and of man-in-it?—into its onto-*epistemologic* worries: what is the "beginning" of man's thought, man's comprehending of comprehension itself? (And in this, Kabbalah joins the speculative thought of any age and any place on earth.)

The Light-before-light—"Splendours," *zahzahat*—is the hidden radiation, the "magic" body, in the hidden, concealed Infinity. But how can Light be a hidden light if not, inclusively, being the in-being's no-being; a no-thing, complete nothingness, *Ayin-ha-gamur,* thus any thing's about-being: Kabbalah's Divine Vagueness, at once Light, Flame, Sound, Root, and Speech—the never-heard-as-yet speech, unspoken still, to-be-spoken, to be achieved as Letter-Number-Name-Naming, the "beginning of being."

And the Light-before-within-Light is all this, at once, forever: in the fullness-vagueness of mind-rock's working. It is Infinity's, God's, future-past-present acting: finity. It is the tension of *about to be immediacy,* the birth of touch, of the presence of adhesion—the two before one; it is Immediacy-seizure, the seed in the soil of man's deepest

and hidden aspiration (Kant, Spinoza, Hegel). In Kabbalah, it is the
birth-by-touch—the seed in the rock—of the Light's two other lights-
aspirations—or *mizuzah*—the birth of the three-one Light that is the
"root of the roots" of the three upper *Sefirot*-Manifestations: *Kether*
(crown), *Hokhmah* (wisdom), *Binah* (Supernal Mother), (Kabbalah's
first triad), the nine *Sefirot* together forming Kabbalah's three sefirotic
triads—a multi-branched plant of life watered by the maternal waters
of *Hokhmah* and *Binah*, the tenth, the last *Sefirah*, *Malkhuth* (that is,
Shekhinah), being the culmination-beginning of all of them, at once
unique and one-within-all-of-them. (It was this triadic structure of Kabbalah's meditation that fascinated so—and so erroneously—the trini-
tary Christians of the pro-Kabbalah sixteenth century—a Pico della
Mirandola, a Ficino and many others.)

   And the oscillating *tension* of the Plenitude-Vagueness is precisely this immediacy-seizure: when the unseizable, uncorporeal *infinity* of pleasure, in all its unseizable, unlocatable Plenitude-Vagueness,
as one of the sages of Safed, Israel Sarug[15] would have it, is seized by
its total transfer into corporeality and location, into the finity of pain.

   The finity of pain substituted for the infinity of pleasure: would
this be the meaning inherent in the name "long-faced one," "forbearing one," borrowed from the biblical "long-suffering one," given in the
Zohar to the primeval heavenly Being, Arikh Anpin, the "vast Counte-
nance," of the first Sefirah? And would the same meaning be hidden in
the semi-legendary episode told in one of the biographies of Baal Shem
—half myth, half fact—the fantastic *Shibche-Ha-Besht* being the
earliest?

   "On one such mysterious journey [his preaching and healing
journeys], the Besht, accompanied by his Gentile driver Alexis and a
young man then living at Brodi, set out for a long ride to the city of
Pozna. On the way, they stopped at a humble house near the edge of an
unknown village. The Besht and his Jewish companion went inside,
while Alexis, on the Besht's orders, remained sound asleep in the car-
riage—as was his custom on these mysterious travels.

   "'Inside sat an old man, his complete body covered with wounds
and scales. . . . When the old man saw the Besht, he was most joyful,
immediately ran to him offering his hand and saying "Welcome, my
teacher.". . . They then went into another room, staying there a half
hour. They then came out, and took leave of one another.'"[16]

   When returning from Pozna, Baal Shem told the bewildered

young Jew who accompanied him that the old man was the Messiah—
for each generation has the actual Messiah, to reveal himself if the generation is worthy. The idea of the Messiah being an old wounded man
appears in Talmud.

The Judaic passion of interiority never ceases to be passion—
India's satisfaction-appeasement of Atman-Brahman's "kiss" is never
Kabbalah's. Yet it too is there: Plenitude-Vagueness is this precisely.
For *Eyn-Sof*'s act of Substitution is an act of pain—*zimzum is "the
long-suffering one," is, so some kabbalists dared to think, the Error
Divine itself.* But tension, mind's passionate tension, "the beginning of
being" in a thought, is the simultaneity of two opposite directions (all
tension being from the first the two-before-one): the Judaic ascent to
substitution—creation *ex nihilo*—is at the same time the descent
deeper and deeper (despair! light now!) unrelentingly into the deep of
the before-the-before of creation, the before of the act of *zimzum* itself;
it is mind's plunge into the mobile world of correspondences and inter-
connections. This is, precisely, Kabbalah's world of Emanations, the
ten *Sefirot*, each and all, in each and all of the four worlds of Existence,
"the four Shadows" of the Hidden Name: the world of Emanation, the
Azilutic world (*Olam-ha-Aziloth*): the *Olam-ha-Binah*, the world of
Creation; the Yeziratic world (*Olam-ha-Yezirah*), the world of Formation; the Asiahtic world (*Olam-ha-Asiah*), the world of Action and of
Shells—material shells—called also *Olam-ha-Clipoth*; this is the
world of evil spirits and their ten own Emanations.

Correspondence—the self-intertwining of the manifested-concealed *Ayin*, of infinity's withdrawal "from itself to itself"—is made
one, one process-genesis, with its opposite, Substitution.

Total Substitution, total Correspondence, total Solitude, total
Solidarity.

And still deeper: the ten *Sefirot* that in-emanate from the act of
substitution—*zimzum*—are all part of infinity's dialectical in-tension:
the *Sefirot* descend into each other in unending about-to-be-corporeal,
self-echoing reflections, correspondences all. These are the famous "aspects," *behinot*, of the *Sefirot*, as the greatest Judaic dialectician, Moses
Cordovero of Safed, saw and described them: the *Sefirah Kether* (supreme crown, the first, still not manifested *Sefirah*)-within-*Kether*-
within-*Kether, Hokhmah*-within-*Hokhmah*-within-*Hokhmah, Binah*-
within-*Binah*-within-*Binah*, and so on with all the ten Powers. And
each and all of the *Sefirot*, instantaneously, together with their infinite

"aspects-beginnings"—the *behinot*—plunge into the *Sefirot* before and after a given *Sefirah*—each action of each aspect being a repetition at once of the creation of infinite correspondences and of creation *ex nihilo*, *zimzum*, the act of infinity's concealment, its withdrawal into itself, into Nothingness.

And in the interior of these onto-cosmological "aspects" Kabbalah reveals-conceals mind's own "aspects" of the *reshit*, the beginning: the birth of mind's onto-epistemological *behinot*, the birth of a sensation, of a perception, of an idea.

Then, still deeper vibrating-oscillating irradiations create more subtle correspondences: Cordovero's (and already, in embryo, the thirteenth-century kabbalist Gikatilla's) "channels," the channels between all Sefirotic "aspects."

And behold now! The *interruption* of the channels' back-and-forth-flow within the life-stream of each creature is the only *sin* Kabbalah admits—the evil of the "left hand" of God, *sitra ahra*, mind's world of interruptions. It is the interruption of the "descent on behalf of the ascent," the world of Lilith the beautiful demoness, the Lady of the world of the "broken vessels'" scattered shards, *klippod*, as well as of Light's sparks kept there as yet imprisoned—beautiful Lilith, pitiful Lilith, the killer of all that is, all those who are to be born, the killer of her own lovers, poets whose memory of the first spark is not hers—Lilith the oblivious one who did not, who does not know it.

And so the real (because so passionate) descent into pre-creation's tension continues: nothing is "stable," nothing is "established" in Kabbalah; neither Infinity itself nor its manifestations-powers, the *Sefirot* themselves.

In Kabbalah's meditation, to the splendours of Infinity's Light that shone into the primeval point's, *zimzum*'s, vacated space (*tehiru*), the new ray of *Eyn-Sof*'s Light was added. (Added? would then the act of creation be an unfinished act? Would this be the very root of the primeval divine Error?) This compounded Light (Light-speech-name-letter-number) then created its own—the same-else!—vessels-containers, the *kelim*, the vessels of Light's manifestations—Light themselves.

And when—so the meditation of Luria, Safed's "Lion," continues—the accumulated light-reality-truth became too heavy for the vessels to contain it, the vessels broke (*Shevirat-Ha-Kelim:* "the Breaking of the Vessels").

And Infinity's first Form, the manifested-concealed image of the primeval man-cosmos, Adam Kadmon of the Gnosis, was broken also. Then (then-now, as Kabbalah would have it), in the interior—the passionate spark-preparing interior of the rock-mind—new Faces in-emerged, in-emanated, the *parzufim*,[17] "Faces" of Infinity-Nothingness (*Ayin*), that changed and yet reestablished the infinite "aspects," the *Sefirot*-and-*behinot* themselves. Faces, new Names: the first *Sefirah*, *Kether*, *Ayin* itself, became now=then the *parzuf Arikh-Anpin*, the "long-faced one," the indulgent or the forbearing one; the *Sefirot Hokhmah* and *Binah* "became" the *parzufim* of *Abba* and *Imma*, Father and Mother, which "serve as the supreme archetype for the procreative 'coupling' (*zivvug*) which, in its metaphorical aspect of face-to-face contemplation (*histakkelut panim-be-fanim*) is the common root of all intellectual and erotic unions."[18]

And the broken form of Adam Kadmon then became the perfect Form: the balance-scales (*matkela*) that created the perfect balance, man-and-woman at once—the only stability in Kabbalah and the only aspiration.

And it is then that upon these new Faces of reconstruction, the *parzufim*, the main supports of the redeeming correction of Error—upon the deepest deep of the Great Sea, "the Maternal Waters," the Shekhinah—that the seal of the first Sound-Light, Sound-Speech, the letter-voice, *Yod*,[19] the first letter of the concealed Name, the Tetragrammaton, descended.

And this descent was the descent of *Hokhmah*'s most concealed power: the seal of judgment's attribute of mercy, *Rahamim*.

And thus Torah was born. Torah: the grown and now maternal Secret Woman, the paternal Ancient of Ancients, Adam Kadmon.

And here also *zimzum*'s act of substitution and the opposite act of correspondence and of interconnection (the dialectical dynamics of all and each of the *Sefirot*) were joined: the glory and the uniqueness of Judaic meditation is in this. And this glory—*koved*—is the highest seat in the heaven-ascending Chariot of the prophets—*Merkabah*—where Shekhinah, the Secret Woman, the Presence, sits.

It is unique and it is Judaic because the whole complexity of Jewish meditation—the Kabbalah—is this simple vision of the one source: the one river and one "great sea" and one great tree of life: the moral law of the Torah—Shekhinah revealed. The Law. For Torah's passion, the Judaic passion of interiority, is the passion of removing from the authority of mind, judgment—*Din*—the rigor and severity of judgment alone, by separating from it and at once uniting with it the redeeming "balance-scales," the restituting, restoring *Rahamim*, mercy —Shekhinah's very being: the Judaic passion of Justice, "the action of Justice beyond the limits of strict Justice," as the "loyal" Hasidei Ashkenaz of the twelfth century wanted it [20] so ardently and so dangerously.

And all this, all the preparatory steps for mind-rock's creation of the spark, the comprehending of comprehending, and all the Error-and-Correction (*tikkun*) of the Creation itself, the genesis-achievement, the Vagueness-Plenitude, of the sefirotic universe itself, all this is nothing but one same-else momentum: the immediacy, the total seizure, of Adam Kadmon's—Man's—real Form:

Din-Rahamim, finity-infinity, man-woman, the Presence.

*   *   *

Kabbalah's vision: the immediacy of metaphysical "seizure" as genesis-achievement, and the Judaic vision: Justice as genesis-achievement, as idea-and-action at once, are one and the same thing. *Zimzum* = "justice-beyond-justice."

And this immediacy and this identity are one, again, with mind's seizure, at the bottom of its own depths, of its own primeval, concealed being, the "pure" sensation, mind's simple, unseizable first spark: the sensation-heat, sensation-cold, sensation-shock, sensation-green, sensation-blue—sensations each and all lost as "nothingness," *Ayin*, as infinity, in their total immediacy and unpredictability, found, possibly, as their same-else in the traces of them, in the fleeting, mirroring corporeality of an impression-copy.

Yet the "pure" sensation—*Ayin*, the body-mind's spark—has always been there. And I heard here what I said once already long before the journey started,[21] "Indeed . . . this elemental spot of our innermost self—we call it *sensation*, or the immediate direct reflex of flesh-and-mind's awakening—is unseizable because it is unretainable as a presence. . . . because when occurring it cannot but be total coextension with my body—as pleasure is—a total presence of adherence, with no possible overlapping room or margin there for the consciousness's seizing. It is infinity. (It is thus finity at the same time. . . . because, ironically, infinity becomes exhaustible in the very attempt to seize it physically: 'We shall die, finish—I cannot die, finish, I.')

"A sensation—the thatness, the suchness of it, the whole of it, the sensation-cold, the sensation-roughness, the sensation-loneliness, the sensation-volume, the sensation-angle, the sensation-fall—is always a *past*, a lost, sensation. It can, of course, be retained or normally reconstructed—as an approximative semblance—by the mediate activity of our memory: as a fugitive yet 'faithful' *impression.* But man— and here it is finally, the first-born move of his freedom!—chooses folly, chooses this: that he can at will possess, seize the unseizable wholeness, the thatness of a sensation, by the power—spontaneous if arbitrary—of a substituted testimony-object, any possible but *immediately witnessing* object, as such a ready-to-be object-artifact: this flower, this 'abnormally' broken line, this 'geometry' of a configuration in sound, in smell, in visceral touch. . . . Obviously *this* any-artifact, *this* any-object-of-art—my body's object, my pain, not otherwise, not elsewhere.

"Sensation, the way of substitution, the way of solitude . . . But another way is open to man: impression, the way of correspondence, of solidarity. When we 'remember' a sensation we lose it as an actuality in us, but we gain an added sense of correspondence with the world outside. For the unseized sensation is reconstructed—remembered— only as a trace, a brain trace interconnected—and only thus concretized —with other sensation-traces. The impression is the ever-changing correspondence between such a trace-sensation bunching—let us call it here the trace of a wound in mind's flesh—and its apparently incessant source of wounding, the so-called natural-empirical world around us. Impression is always a form of such a correspondence. And what we call 'naturalism' in art, which is always, more or less, an 'impressionism,' is this.

"But the correspondence between the trace of sensation and its source gives to man only assurance—not certainty—of an actual presence. Only that presence itself could give us certitude: the total identity of a present sensation, the presence of adherence in it. And man wants certainty. Identity is folly, is impossible, because sensation as presence is impossible—is unseizable. But man wants identity and the impossible and the unseizable, come what may, at the price and risk of his sanity. ('The supreme degree of the doctrine of the Divine Unity is the denial of the Divine Unity.')[22] This is man's essential, metaphysical despair and the creativeness of the despair."[23]

And again I heard here, as I did once before, my own asking:

"The sensation-blue. This precise sensation-blue, how could it be, just be, a presence, an actuality, total and mine, in exclusion, at a certain, however fleeting point of psyche-halt, of all other actualities, if, at the same time as it was given to me, and without losing its character of simple, pure sensation *of* blue, it was not also a sort of authentication, a lyrical verification of blue; in other words, if that simple sensation-blue was not in itself and by itself the evidence of its own, *self-transcending* significance or value; therefore, if it was not also a *moral*—chosen as good—*idea* of blue? The sensation-blue and the idea-blue are reversible in the depth of our visual labour. The entire poetry of our world, visible and invisible as yet . . . is there; all the meaning of beauty, therefore, of history, of thought and meditation is there. . . ."[24]

⋆ ⋆ ⋆

And then I asked myself again: How could the rock hide its spark-to-be? How could the mind reach the hidden spark's spot? What was the way or the ways the mind-rock had found in itself to follow? And I heard myself saying:

In Kabbalah, the primeval, hidden tension contains two directions, two ways both opposite to each other and connected, interwoven with each other, made manifest when the infinity of Tension has been totally transferred into, substituted by, the finity of the initial-ultimate point, the point-act of *zimzum.*

And one way in Kabbalah was the way of the point's expansion into a perfect all-encompassing circle—the perfect stability of the Perfect Man, *Adam Kadmon,* and the other way that of the forever-to-be-perfected, spiralling, multi-directed, multi-pointed, mobile line—the sefirotic limbs of Adam Kadmon—numbers, lights, names, and their "magic" combinations.

And so, exactly so, are mind's two ways of penetration and search: the way that leads to the *immediacy of touch,* and the way to the *mediacy of concept.*

And I heard myself saying again that nothing in man is one, everything is two from the start to the end. Man is two-oneness. The "crisis," uninterrupted and historically growing in complexity, of creative opposition and creative interlace is man's painful and rewarding "normalcy.". . . And so it is with all human communication and conviction, historical and individual. There are always *two* opposite-inter-laced ways and methods—never only one!—carrying to us what we either accept or reject as "proof."

The one is the way, the method, that emerges, lit by man's *category of relation*, from the still hidden recesses of what vaguely we name *intuition*—this treasure house of unlimited possibilities of choice—and leads through a series of determining facts, through the linkages of mutual, factual influences, to the acts of observation, description, demonstration and finally conviction and "proof." It is the way of connections and dialectics: the way of sight, of concept.

And opposite it, the other way, the way of immediacy, of no-way thus, with no propelling intuition or category of relation within its origins—but naked relation as such and at once, immediate, a *presence of adherence*—an event-attitude, a two-before-one *touch*, image-touch, image-flesh: the witness, the *proving without proof.*[25]

And then I remembered having added this also:[26] "Perhaps it would be true to say, as is urged today, that two elemental—and inseparable—factors build up the very condition of our normal thinking and knowing—thus, perhaps, of our creation. To begin with, the so-called form-giving, Kantian schema-bearing activity of the mind. Not a part-to-whole grouping activity, but whole-in-part grasp: the *whole* of a thing—the in-ordered whole—silhouetted, as it were, by the direction, the directive order of growth, followed by any given concrete part of the *schematic*—abstracted—whole. This immediate seizing of an ordered wholeness—already its evaluation or judgment according to Kant, Merleau-Ponty's *sens*—is no mere approximate definition of purely intuitive knowledge. It is an in-herent, living, concrete necessity of mind. It is, just is. Hence its 'objectivity.' Nevertheless its function, its maturation into a real symbol-concept-object, is dependent on another function, not immediate or immediately *given* as the first is: the mind's urge to use images: Cassirer's 'the human mind is an image-needing one.'[27] The mind adds—constructs, creates?—the image to the elemental schema or form, the elemental abstracting.

"Now, what I suggest is that in the visual, or rather 'visionary' modality of human awareness and creativity, there is a reverse in the order of our *possession* of these factors, and that this reverse of the order or precedence between them would account for the rejection of the visionary as 'abnormal,' unintelligible, by the 'normal' modality of thought, the thinking in symbols-concepts. It is the *image* that is given

to us at the start in our visual knowing: its undeniable presence, immediate, convincing, unchangeable and whole—the flesh of it. The
visionary image is the visitation; it is given to us *without us*; it comes
and we are possessed by it—just as in the normal, verbal universe we
are possessed by the immediate presence, the givenness, the visitation
of the forms, the schemata (and the only 'speculation,' it seems to me,
that I allow myself here is to separate temporarily, for comprehension's
sake, what is in existence inseparable: the visual from the verbal, etc.).
It is the form, the schema-meaning, that takes the place of the image in
our visional conditioning of thought. What the eye-in-brain creates
there is the form, the schema, the abstraction itself and not the image.
The image-givenness first and the form-need or form-urge next would
be the proper visionary order of precedence. Here that which we possess fully—which is our visual sanity and normalcy—is the form, the
schema; that which we are possessed by—our givenness, our *sickness*,
our *folly*—is the image given to us and not to be made to be, the image-
flesh, the image-hallucination."[28]

And: "The visually given, inescapable birth-event as image-
touch (the image de-formed, the *Image-la-Folle*, the Witness-substitu-
tion, the birth of eye's monster, of the new, the birth of style), and then
added to it, the form-needed *lucidity* of mind (the birth of the 'natural'
in the eye, intuition's facticity, impression-correspondence)—this is
what the modern Japanese poet Yoni Noguchi named the 'visionary
circumstance of mind.'"[29]

Lucidity now confines the untamable Folle!

Precisely: the schema-lucidity in Picasso's monsters, in Klee's,
in Miró's, in Giacometti's, in Dubuffet's, in Kabbalah's.

"(And we can thus partly explain why it is, historically, that
mysticism, which is simply and normally a visionary—a visual—experience through and through, has been rejected, despised, and often
relegated to the world of insanity by the 'verbal'—verbally ordered
world that normally uses the help of imagination, of visions narrated,
but not actually embodied.)"[30]

⋆

⋆   ⋆

⋆

In Kabbalah, Judgment's image-concept is judgment with mercy, *Din and Rahamim*, and Judgment's image-touch is judgment-mercy, *Din-Rahamim*, fused together in Creation's Plenitude-Vagueness: *Din-via-Rahamim, Rahamim-via-Din*, man-*via*-woman, woman-*via*-man, Shekhinah, the Presence of Righteousness.

Such also the Plenitude-Vagueness of any sensation, of any perception, as, in Kabbalah, of any aspect-power of *Hokhmah*. When Shekhinah, the Secret Woman, is identified with Kenesset Israel, the *community of Israel* as the community of the righteous only (and Islam's inheritance of this in the sacredness, universality and righteousness, of its Community of Believers, the *Ummat-as-Islam*), this identification acquires meaning on all levels of human existence and creativity: it means that the "moral imperative"—the non-mysterious "mystery" in Torah's, in Light's creation *ex nihilo*, in mind's creation *ex nihilo*—is the very non-mysterious mystery concealed-manifested in any object, in any artifact of man's creation *ex nihilo*.

The point-spark—*zimzum*—in Kabbalah's meditation, at once root of the finite, encompassing circle and root of an ever-continued spiralling line, and Paul Klee's "birth of the black arrow," his arrow-spark, arrow-direction, are one and the same.

Paul Klee, a "goy" who never knew what the Jewish Midrashic-Haggadic Kabbalah had said in words, yet who knew what Kabbalah knew. Who said: "In the world of physical reality every ascent must be followed by a descent at the moment at which the gravitational pull of the earth overcomes the ascending energy of the rudder. The physical curve thus ends as a perpendicular line (theoretically in the center of the earth).

"In contrast . . . a cosmic curve frees itself more and more from the earth in infinite motion, to fulfill itself freely in a circle or at least an ellipse."[31] And . . . "this direction determines either a gradual liberation from the center through freer and freer motions, or an increasing dependence on an eventually destructive center.

"This is the question of life and death. . . ."[32]

"Revelation: that nothing that has a start can have infinity.

"Consolation: a bit farther than customary!—than possible?

"Be winged arrows, aiming at fulfillment and goal, even though you will tire without having reached the mark."[33] Paul Klee: who created *ex nihilo* the corporeality—Klee's image-touch-concept at once—

23. PAUL KLEE: *Man Teetering on Stilts.*

24. PAUL KLEE: *Quarry at Ostermündigen.*

25. PAUL KLEE: *Magicians in Dispute.*

26. PAUL KLEE: *Heron.*

of an abstract direction-motion, the erect black arrow—the centred

object of his "devotion to small things"—ejected from within the
womb of his white nothingness-plenum (*Ayin*) (*see Plate 19*); Klee's
"white-in-white" ("the given white, much-too-much-seen and tire-
some white...noticed by the eye with little sensation...")[34] in
whose belly—my belly—the very increase of tension, the white's "descent on behalf of the ascent," "from itself to itself" (*Ayin*) has created
the opposition-correspondence of two directions-curves: the more and
more-and-more of tension, the more-and-more and more of white, the
less and less and less of white, the more and more of its opposite, the
black, till the resulting final mixture of two opposed about-to-be bodies,
the tense white, and its same-else, the tense black, culminate in the
full corporeity of a new, a first, thing, a "monster," the black arrow.

Here is Klee's primeval infinity-substituting point—*zimzum*—
the root of roots of all his in-emanations: the concealed-manifested
"universe of discourse" of Klee's line-colour-meaning, the *sefirotic*
Plenitude-Vagueness of his imagery (*Plates 23, 24, 25, 26*).

But Klee also said: "Passing on to infinite movement, where the
actual direction of movement becomes irrelevant, I first *eliminate* the
arrow. Through this act heating and cooling-off, for instance, become
one. *Pathos (or tragedy) turns into ethos* [italics mine], which encom-
passes energy and counter-energy within itself."[35] For Klee knew the
primeval Error and the primeval Restoration (*tikkun*) and Torah's
"moral imperative" of the Drama and of the Presence: Klee knew, his
line-colour knew the beauty and the lure of despair; they knew how
"Hope creates / From its own wreck the thing it contemplates." His was
the poet's meditation:

> *Open thyself, thou gate in the depths,*
> *Cell underground, release me*
> *who senses light.*
> *And bright hands come and seize me,*
> *and friendly words are spoken joyously:*
> *Forth, you beautiful pictures, wild beasts,*
> *spring forth from thy cage*
> *that fingers may glide lovingly*
> *on flaming hide.*

And all is one as once in God's garden:
day and night,
and sun and splendor of stars.
(In the paradise of those trembling with poetry.) [36]

         ⋆   ⋆   ⋆

And just as the road of Origins and Loyalty, the road of Purity, ended at the "pure" *shtieble*—the Grass! the Cow! the Woman!—of Baal Shem's great-grandson, so the road of Meditation ended here. It ended behind the vacated space-point (*tehiru-zimzum*) of infinity's withdrawal into itself—the no-thingness—and the memory of the "pure" Presence there—the first spark, the Shekhinah! It ended behind the "Garment"—*malbush*—of both the visionary (the world of the image-touch, of *Image-la-Folle*, image-substituted) and the conceptual (the world of the image-concept, image-proof-correspondence); behind both the perfect finite circle (man's solitude in the cosmos) and the never final multi-directed line (man's solidarity in the cosmos):

    The end of Kabbalah's and Paul Klee's road—Paul Klee's together with all his visionary-conceptual companions through all ages and all places on earth.

    The road of Meditation ended here in a sudden, sharp and unexpected curve. And continued: the very same road with a brusquely changed direction. And I changed its name. I called it, when I saw it and entered it, the road of Companions.

4
The Road of Companions

THE ROAD I ENTERED made such a sharp detour that, after a few steps along it, the other road started to disappear from view. And I was left with a feeling, a melancholy and greedy feeling, of someone— an old, still hopeful gold searcher—who fills his "pan" to its full capacity with the alluvial, gold-carrying earth, plunges it into the stream, shaking and twisting it there vigorously, and then watches the pan be emptied, washing out its dark, opaque content of "pay dirt" with only a few precious gold grains, coarse gold nuggets, remaining at its bottom —my golden residual memories of past meditations. A few rough golden grains-memories.

And the first one my eye met, a most remote, half-forgotten memory-grain (how could I expect it here?) was the trembling beauty and bliss of a red passionate winter rose, trembling on its long stem one rainy late afternoon against the outer wall of Granada's Isabellan Royal Chapel in distant Andalusia.

Frail, delicate and distant, erect and tenacious, passionate red rose! Such I remembered her now, withstanding the windy onrush of all the evils, human and not human, Pandora's opened vase had once let loose—greed-*via*-indifference, cruelty-*via*-indifference, self-justification-*via*-indifference leading them all. And I remembered their challenging her right to be there, her frailty to be the bliss there. And I remembered then her answer—a frail, delicate, erect and tenacious answer.

And this was the second golden, gold-lighted grain in the gold-searcher's pan—my second memory-grain of the meditation road: Rabbi Nachman of Bratislaw telling us, answering all of us: "The Lord, blessed be He, has created the world as an absolute solitude and the man in it as an absolute solitude. And He created this solitude of the world as an absolute solidarity, and the solitude of man as an absolute solidarity. And He gave to this absolute, the only absolute, and to this union, the only union, a name. He called it Tenderness. For tenderness is solitude-solidarity. And He made this first and this only absolute and this first and this only union into one being, a frail, tenacious, passionate living being.

"He made Tenderness the last, the tenth *Sefirah*, *Sefirah Malkhuth*, the tenth *Sefirah* containing all ten *Sefirot*—the Secret Woman's, the Shekhinah's home. And the secret, metaphysical Tenderness of the 'beginning of being' in the world and in man. It is the primeval force, the 'root of roots'—frail, passionate, tenacious and convincing—that made the pre-creation's 'judgment alone' bend toward 'mercy alone' and bind them together, judgment-*via*-mercy, mercy-*via*-judgment now, infinity's act of self-concealment-contraction, the very act of creation *ex nihilo*, *zimzum*, the act of substitution and correspondence.

"And more: Tenderness is the primeval divine Error already-to-be-redeemed by itself. For Tenderness is the solitude-solidarity, the plenitude-vagueness in and of the world, in and of the man, that made the incorporeal judgment-*via*-mercy, mercy-*via*-judgment to be the corporeality—the body—of the man-*via*-woman, of the woman-*via*-man.

"Righteousness," thus ended the zaddik Nachman, "is Tenderness: the 'moral imperative,' the spirit made body—the Shekhinah."

Of all the great planetary, private and collective meditations it was the Judaic meditation that made its "moral imperative"—Justice as "the action beyond the limits of strict Justice"[1]—to be the very root of the "beginning of being": not in the stars, not in destiny, not even in God, but as *amor intellectualis Dei,*" the intellectual love of God, this concealed-manifested gift from the pure Jewish passion of interiority to the world at large. The Judaic meditation is thus not Judaic only; it is Judaic-*via*-universal, it is universal-*via*-Judaic, universal, ubiquitous on *all levels* of existence and human action: the "moral imperative" [would this be my closest memory, the last residual grain of gold at the bottom of the pan?] is the non-mysterious mystery in the Torah, in the three-one Light's creation, the "moral imperative," the non-mysterious mystery in mind's creation; the mysterious mystery concealed-manifested in any object, in any artifact of man's creation *ex nihilo.*

"Art is the shelter of justice." I heard myself saying it once.[2] The point—the spark hidden in the rock—the finite circle of Kabbalah's meditation, the never-finished line of Kabbalah's meditation, and the finite circle=the never-finite line in Paul Klee's birth of an arrow-spark, arrow-directive, are one and the same "root of roots."

Art is the secret metaphysical Woman, the Shekhinah; the Shekhinah, the secret metaphysical Woman is art: a frail, delicate and distant, erect, tenacious passionate winter rose in distant Spain—a frail, delicate, distant erect and tenacious argument. . . .

Who was it, suddenly coming toward me? "Is that you, Giovanni?" I said. "What are you doing here, Giovanni di Paolo,[3] a total stranger here?"

GIOVANNI DI PAOLO

I heard a great roar. It came from where you are. I knew what it was, and so, my memory attracting me, I went there. A stranger, true, I am now of here and of now. I heard a great roar—cataclysmic descent? ascent? —of the elements. I heard again the formation, through fire, air, water and solid dust, of the cosmos and of the soul. And then, the formation of the tormented solid crust of our revolving earth and the formation of the solid crust of what my revolving soul was formed for and by. The formation of my art: the roaring—cosmic—up-tension, the roaring—cosmic—up-pressure of the molten innermost magma piercing through the thickness of its cooling off and solidified surface, ejecting there in convulsed blocks of molten metallic matter the vertiginous summits of its igneous "plutonic" mountain-rocks!

How perpetual is indeed the memory on earth of the terrestrial strain of its sufferings and tensions! Here: the primeval tension of fire, of air, of water and globe-in-depth-encircling solid rock, this tension growing, pressing, growing increasingly—more and more tension, more and more contracting, compressing, hardening of the volcanic matter—reducing, finally, the unseizable, the incommensurable total of the asymmetrical and substantial massing to the seizable, measurable—symmetrical and structural—unity and finality of a crystal.

And the crystallized igneous rock foundations—from the smooth transparency of hard glassy rock to the coarseness of hard granite—gave birth to their last-born child, the most condensed, the hardest, the most crystallized of all crystals: the gem-stone, fire, air, water, earth then forming one substance and one structure, one accident and one essence, one action and one value; the unseizable cause one with the seized result: the most precious diamond, ruby and sapphire, emerald, amethyst. . . . I, Giovanni di Paolo, I painted the formation of the precious gem-stone.

I

But Giovanni, you never painted, precisely, or actually, a gem-stone, a diamond, a ruby or a sapphire and an emerald.

GIOVANNI DI PAOLO

Of course. Painter-artisan, humble and competent, of pious icons in fifteenth-century Siena, the unhappy Siena of my time, so humiliated by its political and financial reverses, so tormented, as all city-states in Italy of that time were, by social unrest leading to the rule of despots, emotionally and intellectually still living with the more than a century-old memories of the Black Death and the resulting moral duality of extreme, dissolute hedonism on one hand and on the other the extreme religiosity and austerity, belligerent and ardent in, say, a St. Catherine or a Capellani, suave and ardent in a St. Bernardine—how and why would I know how and why to paint the formation and the growth of a gem-stone—a strange, unexpected "monster"—and the distant meaning of this?

I

[Aside: Crystal—crystallization: the "beginning of being"—*zim-zum!* . . .]

GIOVANNI DI PAOLO

It took my being your road companion here, it took your twentieth century itself, to know that "a painter paints what he does not paint,"[4] that what a painting wants to say—precisely that what is the beautiful is at once what is the true and what is the good—is not expressed in and by its line's conduct, its colour's structure, its composition's promise, but in the very line itself, in the colour itself, in the composition itself. It

27. GIOVANNI DI PAOLO: *Madonna and Child, with Four Saints.*

28. AMBROGIO LORENZETTI: *The Presentation of Christ in the Temple.*

29. GIOVANNI DI PAOLO: *The Presentation of Christ in the Temple.*

took a twentieth-century thinker, Bertrand Russell, to say to me that "every language has, as Mr. Wittgenstein says, a structure concerning which, *in the language*, nothing can be said, but that there may be another language dealing with the structure of the first language, and having itself a new structure, and that to this hierarchy of languages there may be no limit. Mr. Wittgenstein would, of course, reply that his whole theory is applicable unchanged to the totality of such languages. The only retort would be to deny that there is any such totality";[5] and still another to say the retort itself is not total. The unseizable, perhaps nonexistent totality or plenitude is possibly to be seized, concretized, and substituted by a concrete fragment of it, here the loss of something in the language so transferred into another; and it is precisely this very loss in one that is the gain in the other: the gain of the awareness that plenitude and vagueness are made of the same being.

I painted pious, tormented icons when I painted the torment of the precious gem's birth and formation. And I painted Creation's divine Error—of tension and confusion—and the presence as well as the present in it of redemption-correction: tension's release and liberation, the crystal-clear gem.

I

[Aside: *Image-la-Folle*, appear! Here, over here!]

I believe you, Giovanni di Paolo. Can I forget your convincing "proving without proof" when one day I saw in the Uffizi your Madonna with Child and Saints (*Plate 27*)—the heavy, tormented border of her mantle spreading in oceanic wave-curves their compact, fleshy plenitude? Who else in your time painted such a condensed and tense plenitude? (Would that be the reason for your predilection for small and *condensed* icons, your predellas, your panels surrounding a central scene in your altarpieces, as well as for your technical-expressive ability to paint them?) Not Gentile da Fabriano, whom you admired and enjoyed so much. Not Sassetta, for whose crystalline transparencies you had such keen fellow-feeling.

[A moment of silence]

The tormented summits and the floors of your architectures! When, modelled faithfully on Ambrogio Lorenzetti's "Presentation in the Temple" you painted in your own Presentation (*Plates 28, 29*), so faithfully identical to Ambrogio's, the three minuscule sculptured figurines on the upper balustrade, how different from Ambrogio's corresponding

30. GIOVANNI DI PAOLO: *St. Catherine of Siena Receiving the Stigmata.*

31. GIOVANNI DI PAOLO: The Branchini *Madonna and Child.*

three are your intentionally contorted, almost convulsed bodies! And the tormented arrangement of the three differing directions on the floor's pavement! And in your Saint Catherine of Siena Receiving the Stigmata (*Plate 30*), the fugue-like torment of the columns and the vaulting: unforgettable *Image-la-Folle*!

GIOVANNI DI PAOLO

Yet, it is the release, the redemption of the torment-error of our planet's crust, of our inner being's crust, that I wanted to tell: the secret of the precious crystal.

I

[Aside: Crystallization. The first crystal—the "beginning of being," *zimzum*!]

GIOVANNI DI PAOLO

. . . The crystal-gem, tenderness born among the craggy rocks, the rocky veins and cavities, among the detrital remains, or deposits—gravels, sands, ashes—testimony to cosmic struggles, to the birth of earth's crust, its maturation, disintegration and weathering—light-treasuring tenderness of their totally transferred and liberated selves: the rolling crystals-gems; the hardest one, the diamond, this cubic quintessential-ized carbon crystal; the ruby, the sapphire, the most precious crystal-lized alumina or corundum, the emerald, and the softer amethyst and topaz found in granitic rocks. . . .

The diamond! Fire-air-water-earth embracing and sheltering crystal, closest witness of the Drama! I painted the cubic-crystalline formation of the diamond.

I

Oh, yes, Giovanni. From your earlier achievements, the sharp-edged, multi-faced adamantine radiations surrounding and supporting your Madonna Branchini (*Plate 31*) to, later on, that most daring communi-cation of yours, the transfer of the gem's arrested drama into the drama of man's inner journey, your Saint John entering the wilderness (*Plate 32*), you were painting, you were telling, the story of the diamond and of its cosmic destiny. Flashes of light, lightnings and fire in a "pure water" diamond, that is what they are, the sharp-angled self-crossing roads of your travelling young Saint John's novel landscape there! (And

32. GIOVANNI DI PAOLO: *St. John in the Wilderness.*

not, as is often suggested, you know, the result of Sienese technical provincialism when compared to the contemporary perspectivist-mathematical discoveries in Florence, embodied in painting in the "correctly" calculated and rendered perspective of a chequered floor. Nor your fifteenth-century Sienese nostalgic attachment to the medieval—Lombard, French—spatial structure and your unwillingness or incompetence to follow those new Florentine pictorial rules. For you knew very well and were very capable of understanding and following a Paolo Uccello, a Domenico Veneziano.)

And when, as an old man, you gave us in your Last Judgment (*Plate 33*) the translucid, cool radiant thinly populated scene of the "Judgment" proper, flanked by the compact, heavy, granitic, almost coarse "Paradise" and "Hell" (*Plates 34–35*), you painted the most transparent of all the gems, lost and found in the debris of rude granitic and carbon rocks. Oh yes! For you never forgot the "tragic sense of history" of the gem's birth and of its separation from that rocky, rude, coarse matrix—carbon, granite, even obsidian: the sudden, angular coarseness of some of your saints, of their silhouettes, their features, the delineation of their hands, hair, the discomfort of their gestures (*Plates 36, 37*).

GIOVANNI DI PAOLO

But: the pallor covering the hidden fire of a ruby, of an emerald, secret, still hidden among other crystalline pebbles . . .

I

That great surprise! the frail yet rocky pallor of your most exalted gem and saint, Saint Catherine and the ruby-and-sapphire hidden lightnings of her uplifted hands receiving the stigmata (*See Plate 30*)—your most exalted gem-to-be, my most exalted gem-to-be!

And what passion had heated and burned the disquieting *agnus dei* red blood of a ruby and changed it into the dark and quieting green of an emerald, as the red of a ruby when heated changes to green, yet, after cooling, returns to its original red fire of a ruby?—what red torment made the sky, the sea, the praying wrecked humanity in your Saint Nicholas of Tolentino rescuing a sinking ship (*Plate 38*) temporarily change this torment into the deep, crystalline, arrested quietude of green?

33. GIOVANNI DI PAOLO: *The Last Judgment.*

GIOVANNI DI PAOLO

One day I gathered and kept in my hand many gems together, a dazzling compact bunch of beatitudes and melodies. . . . A great day!

I

I know, I know. It was your Expulsion from Paradise! (*Plate 39*). And here, no more words, Giovanni. Melodies, perhaps, as you just said. Yes: melodies. Music—crystals of plenitude-vagueness, not words, crystals of precision and limitation.

But—why are you leaving me so suddenly, Giovanni di Paolo? I've not offended you, have I? It would be so sad . . . so unwittingly . . .

[*Left alone, seated on a big stone by the roadside, meditatively*]

. . . Melodies . . . melodies . . .

Have I offended you? Was it my surprised greeting? "Hello, Gio-

vanni di Paolo," I said. "And what are you doing here, a stranger on this road of Companions?" But you explained to me: "I heard a great roar coming from where you are—the roar of the Elements—the birth in the fiery gas, the fiery liquid, the fiery solid, of the hardest of all solids, the crystal-gem. So I came here. And here I am of now and of here, your companion."

You said to me later, "I painted the birth of the most precious gems on earth."

Then I said to you, "Giovanni di Paolo, you never painted a ruby, an emerald or a diamond."

"Of course," you answered me, "but I did. It took my coming here to you, it took your twentieth century, to be able to say: 'A painter paints what he does not paint,' and to boldly suggest 'every language has a structure concerning which in the language, nothing can be said

34. GIOVANNI DI PAOLO: *Paradise* (detail from *The Last Judgment*).

35. GIOVANNI DI PAOLO: *Hell* (detail from *The Last Judgment*).

36. GIOVANNI DI PAOLO: *The Assumption.*

37. GIOVANNI DI PAOLO: *St. Jerome.*

38. GIOVANNI DI PAOLO. *Miracle of St. Nicholas of Tolentino.*

39. GIOVANNI DI PAOLO: *Expulsion of Adam and Eve from Paradise.*

. . . but there may be another language dealing with the structure of the first language, and having itself a new structure, and . . . to this hierarchy of languages there may be no limit.'"[6]

That is what you said to me *really*, secretly and intently. . . .

How could I miss it then? I know now. *Your* language—your total existence—total, unseizable, Giovanni di Paolo, has a structure concerning which nothing can be said in your language, but there is another language—my language, my total existence-language . . . etc., etc.

You are here, of now and of here, Giovanni di Paolo—transferred into me with all your loss=my gain: your secret, central obsession, the secret Presence, the gem-stone, whose concrete, finite thingness is the thingless infinity-nothingness's substitution and manifestation. Your central obsession (*l'Image-la-Folle*) in you—in me. Your-my metaphysical tenderness. The Secret Woman. *Shekhinah*. In you, in me. In everyone's creation *ex nihilo*—the secret of poetry: this precise, concrete witness-thing of child's unforgettable unrepeatable experience, an object-idea, an object-feeling, the ripe grape, its translucid juicy taste and smell, the obsession-substitution in Rubens; the birth of a dark pearl in Rembrandt; the miraculous birth of a porcelain in the earlier Goya; the rainbow in Renoir, the birth of the white in a Winslow Homer, of the red in an Eakins; the simple, "banal" and ponderous weight, Cézanne's secret of correspondence-substitution; your precious gem-stone, Giovanni; the birth of sonority, of music in Dosso Dossi. (I did not expect to find here this additional grain of gold, this additional gleam of a golden memory in the memory-searcher's pan!)

The birth of sonority. Dosso Dossi:[7] music, melodies now. Music: that which makes me, a solid, opaque, moving and serene being—me or Ararat's summit at the Deluge—become, fire doing this, a restless liquid, transparent, directed, mobile—me or deluge or tear, or ocean, or stream—and then, fire increased, become gaseous, translucidly light, fulfilled, agitated and explosive—me, the same me, the primeval elemental atom-gas, the bearer of astrophysics' creation-being—bang!—a new being, solid, opaque and serene, severe-and-merciful.

Music: the Giorgionesque Venetian music-secret (*see Plates 4, 5*) of Dosso Dossi . . . The word music and not side-by-side-with, but *via* the word music and *via* the word man in it, the word woman, crystal of plenitude-vagueness, Tenderness: Dosso Dossi's "Circe" (*Plate 3*), the sorceress silencing the leafy dark nature and the men-*via*-beasts in it,

Circe-Orpheus, Circe-Pythagoras, man-*via*-woman, woman-*via*-man—

Shekhinah.

Dosso Dossi, your John the Baptist (*Plate 1*) again, and the polyphonic landscape-madrigal there, and Melissa (*Plate 2*) and the sonorous metamorphosis of the Camera delle Cariatidi in the Villa Imperiale at Pesaro[8] (*Plate 40*) . . .

L'art ne s'élargit pas, il se résume—art is not expansion, it is reduction. Who said it? Who is saying it, so authoritatively and so necessarily here, at this moment of my descriptive expansion and of its—I feel it suddenly—indiscretion? Who among Kabbalah's road companions?

L'art ne s'élargit pas, il se résume. But—is it possible?—it is your voice, Edgar Degas. You, the "pure goy," Jew-hating, ignorant of Jews? Impossible. Yet, it is you. And, of course, you cannot be the ignoring one any more: you are among the dead (as if in Dante's *Divine Comedy*). You know now—I know now—and nobody else knows, perhaps nobody would even wish to know: that Edgar Degas, the late nineteenth-century's great realist painter, the teller of Parisian scenes—his little ballet dancers, his little jockeys and the racehorses, his bathing women, his friends' portraits—was the painter of the secret, silent, invisible Presence.

From reduction to reduction, from in-depth transfer to in-depth transfer—and I know it now, you know it now and nobody else would know it, would perhaps even wish to know it—you both concealed and manifested this uncorporeal Presence by painting another presence, invisible yet corporeal, the presence of an "astral" body surrounding a painted living being.

Monsieur Degas, you are the painter of the "astral" body—of the moral irradiation, Torah's "moral imperative," aureoling a person's action—at once concealed and revealed either as a corporeal absence-presence, the same-else (this young woman in a millinery shop trying on a hat, trying it on a somebody "else," absent, present, concealed, revealed (*Plate 41*); or an expanding-and-contracting sonorous presence of a colour-language (this young stage singer and her "astral," "moral" body concealed-manifested in the colour polyphony (*Plate 42*).

And who can forget—I cannot!—your "Fallen Jockey" (*Plate 43*). Somebody—the fallen jockey's living drama-being?—has fallen there: the same-else.

40. DOSSO DOSSI: Mural in the Villa Imperiale, Pesaro.

And the "astral" body-portrait of Mme. Olivier Villette's portrait, your little masterpiece (*Plate 44*)! The melancholy, the intimacy of the grey, unfinished, forlorn and closed window to be opened wide somewhere upon bottomless Paris.

And again the same-else Presence in the presence of this tired laundress ironing (*Plate 45*).

Yours, Monsieur Degas, is an oblique universe—oblique, diagonal, off-center, limits-challenging (*Plates 46–49*). Why? Was it because of the Japanese world, oblique through and through, discovered, admired by all your contemporaries? Yes. But in your secret creative will the simple "spatial obliquity" was a *moral* "spatial obliquity"—it was your witness of the Presence, the oblique, the concealed-manifested Presence.

Monsieur Degas, you, the Jew-hater, you were the painter of the Jewish mystical vision of the creation *ex nihilo*—creation through the act of Reduction supreme—the mystery of *zimzum*, the mystery of all creation on all levels of existence. *L'art ne s'élargit pas, il se résume.* From depth-transfer to depth-transfer in total simultaneity and instantaneity of all Creation's and post-Creation's actions, you painted at once the "oblique" limits-challenging off-center act of the primal divine Error and its redemption-correction by the all-containing will of Tenderness, your secret tenderness, your secret, metaphysical woman, Monsieur Degas.

And you know all the connections, the *missing* connections here. I know all the connections here—what will you tell them, those who are not dead already, who do not know them? I would remind them of the story told in your own sacred Book:

> *And the third day there was a marriage in Cana of Galilee; and the mother of Jesus was there:*
>> *And both Jesus was called, and his disciples, to the marriage.*
>> *And when they wanted wine, the mother of Jesus saith unto him, They have no wine.*
>> *Jesus saith unto her, Woman, what have I to do with thee? mine hour is not yet come.*
>> *His mother saith unto the servants, Whatsoever he saith unto you, do it.* [9]

41. EDGAR DEGAS: *At the Milliner's.*

42. EDGAR DEGAS: *The Singer in Green.*

43. EDGAR DEGAS: *Fallen Jockey.*

44. EDGAR DEGAS: *Portrait of Madame Olivier Villette.*

45. EDGAR DEGAS: *The Laundresses.*

46. EDGAR DEGAS: *Dancer with a Bouquet.*

47. EDGAR DEGAS: *Rehearsal on the Stage.*

48. EDGAR DEGAS: *At the Milliner's.*

49. EDGAR DEGAS: *At the Milliner's.*

Please take a seat, Monsieur Degas, beside me on that big flat
stone close to mine. You must be very tired. At your advanced age,
your sight waning away, how could you walk for long hours along the
streets of Paris, today, up the Rue Berthollet to Boulevard Arago and
then along the solitary Rue de la Glacière, there, stopping a moment in
front of the closed entrance of the stuffy dark *mercerie* or the half-open
entrance of the *blanchisserie*—all the secret, ancient tenderness in
your heart. I know it so well: your Paris of greatest and smallest intimacy, Paris at dusk, luminescent pearl, dissolved . . .

Let's rest a while here. We shall watch and wait. Who will pass
by and greet us next?

We shall wait.

I will wait. . . .

Notes

Prologue

1. The Works of Johann Wolfgang von Goethe, IX, *The Tragedy of Faust*, tr. Anna Swanwick (Göttingen ed.; New York: R. F. Stonestreet & Co., 1901), gives the English as follows:

   All of mere transient date
   As symbol showeth;
   Here, the inadequate
   To fulness groweth;
   Here the ineffable
   Wrought is in love;
   The ever womanly
   Draws us above.

2. Dosso Dossi; Giovanni Luteri, called Dosso Dossi (*ca.* 1479–1542), a Ferrarese painter of renown. Pupil, according to Vasari, of Lorenzo Costa. But it was Venetian painting, that of Giorgione above all, which all his life influenced and inspired him.

   He worked for the Dukes of Este; was highly appreciated by them and their sophisticated court. Ariosto was his friend.

   The painting of John the Baptist, executed around 1520, now in the Palazzo Pitti, belongs to the most characteristic and creative period of the artist. With the exception of one modern critic (W. G. Zwanziger, *Dosso Dossi* [Leipzig: Klinkhardt & Biermann, 1911]) this work is ascribed to him, not to his "Romanized" brother, Battista (*see* Felton Gibbons, *Dosso and Battista Dossi* [New Jersey: Princeton University Press, 1968]).

   In 1531, with his brother and assistants, he decorated the splendid palace-castle of Cardinal Clesio, Bishop of Trent, the Castello del Buon Consiglio in Trent, and, *ca.* 1532, the Villa Imperiale in Pesaro. (See note 8 to Chapter 4).

   Dosso Dossi was the typical product of Ferrarese "Mannerist" court art, imbued with the Venetian rather than with the dominant Roman-Florentine aesthetic ideas of the era.

Much is written of late on the sociology and ideology of the sixteenth century's "Mannerism" and its Ferrarese courtly ambience (Jacques Bousquet, *Mannerism* [New York: Braziller, 1964]; Walter Friedlaender, *Mannerism and anti-Mannerism* [New York: Columbia University Press, 1957]; Arnold Hauser, *Mannerism: the crisis of the Renaissance and the origins of modern art* [London: Kegan, Paul, 1965, 2 v.]; Werner L. Gundersheimer, *Ferrara: The Style of Renaissance Despotism* [New Jersey: Princeton University Press, 1973]): feudalism revivified, in its last, "romantic" and "reactionary," decadent aspect, its magic-occultist curiosities, its passion for the *bizarre*—in poetry, theatre (masques), music; music dominating both as the creative-exalted and as a corrosive force: the conceptist artificiality (*à la* twelfth-century *trovar clus* —"find the key"—Provençal poetry) and inventiveness—the polyphonic madrigal, etc.

3. *Yod*: the first letter of the Tetragrammaton. ". . . Y H V H—the 'lost word'—was above all others the 'saving' name in the tradition of Israel. . . ." It is known as the name "of which every consonant reveals and symbolizes one of the four aspects of fundamental degrees of divine all-reality. . . . It was exactly on account of the direct outpouring of divine grace brought about by the invocation of the name Y H V H that the traditional authority in Israel found it necessary, even before the destruction of the second Temple, to forbid the spiritually fallen people to invoke, or even merely to pronounce the tetragrammaton [replaced by the name *Adonai . . .* and *Yah*, the first half of the Tetragrammaton]." (Leo Schaya, *The Universal Meaning of the Kabbalah*, tr. from the French by Nancy Pearson [London: George Allen & Unwin, Ltd., 1971], p. 145.) "Thus the letter *yod . . .* in Y H V H and *Yah*, is revealed on the discursive level as the sacred ideogram of the undifferentiated unity of the ten *Sefiroth* [see note 12 to Chapter 3]—for the *yod* has the numerical value of ten. . . ." *Ibid.*, p. 151.

4. Ludwig Wittgenstein, *Philosophical Investigations*, tr. G. E. M. Anscombe (Oxford: B. Blackwell, 1967), p. 47 (109).

5. *Ibid.*, p. 48 (119).

6. *Ibid.*, p. 80 (198).

7. *Ibid.*, p. 133 (464).

8. *Ibid.*, p. 82 (203).

9. *Ibid.*, p. 53 (138).

10. *Ibid.*, p. 68 (167).

11. *Ibid.*, p. 103 (309).

12. *Ibid.*, p. 113 (358).

13. *Ibid.*, pp. 132–33 (456–57).

14. *Ibid.*, Part II, p. 179.

15. *Ibid.*, p. 181.

16. *Ibid.*, p. 184.

17. *Ibid.*, p. 187.

18. *Ibid.*, p. 196.

19. *Ibid.*, p. 212.

20. Bertrand Russell, Introduction to Ludwig Wittgenstein, *Tractatus Logico-Philosophicus* (London: Routledge & Kegan Paul, Ltd., 1922), p. 23.

21. Wittgenstein, *Investigations*, p. 8.

22. *Ibid.*, p. 5.

2. Shekhinah, or the Road of Purity

1. *See* Léo Bronstein, *Five Variations on the Theme of Japanese Painting* (Freeport, Maine: The Bond Wheelwright Co., for Brandeis University, 1969), p. 347, note 41 (1).

2. *The Songs of the Cowherd*, By Jaydeva, the Bengali twelfth-century poet.

3. Adam Mickiewicz, 1798–1855, regarded generally as the greatest Polish poet, the leader of the romantic movement and the apostle of Polish-Lithuanian national freedom. *Pan Tadeusz*, his masterpiece, was written in 1832–34.

4. Translated from the first lines of *Pan Tadeusz*:

    Litwo! Ojczyzno moja! ty
    jesteś jak zdrowie;
    Ile cię trzeba cenić, ten tylko
    się dowie,
    Kto cię stracił. Dziś
    piękność twą w całej
    ozdobie
    Widzę i opisuję, bo tęsknię
    po tobie.

    by Watson Kirkconnell (New York: The Polish Institute of Arts and Sciences in America, 1962).

5. *Shtieble*: the home of a Hassidic community leader, which was also a house of study, of prayer and of assembly.

6. Israel ben Eliezer, Baal Shem Tov (The Besht): "the Kind Master of God's names." Founder of modern Hassidism (note 21, below) in Eastern Europe. Born *ca.* 1700 in the small town of Okup on the frontier of Volhynia and Podolia. Facts and fiction are in-

terwoven in what has come down to us concerning his life. What seems certain is that he was orphaned in his early childhood and left in utter poverty. When he was six years old, the elders of the community, as required by Talmud, gave him free education (Max Dimont: *Jews, God and History* [New York: Simon & Schuster, 1962]; Rabbi Dr. H. Rabinowicz, *A Guide to Hassidism* [New York and London: Thomas Yoseloff, 1960]). At thirteen he became the teacher's assistant (*behelfer*). Every morning he led young children to *heder* (lit. room), "the common name for the old-fashioned elementary school for the teaching of Judaism. The name first occurs in the 13th century. . . . The age groups were from 3–5, 6–7, and 8–13." (*Encyclopedia Judaica* [Jerusalem–New York: Macmillan Co., 1972], Vol. 8, p. 241.) The legend has it (in the early and venerated biography, *Shibche Ha-Besht*) that he took them through dangerous surrounding woods and to distract them sang with them all the way. Then he was made beadle of the high school (the Bet ha-midrash—see note 13, below). There he kept himself aloof from the students, slept most of the day while they were studying, studied at night: Talmud and Kabbalah. When he was seventeen, an "old bachelor," the communal authorities found him a wife—who died very soon after. He migrated then to a small town near Brodi, the capital of East Galicia. To eke out a lean existence he worked as teacher and as *shohet* (ritual butcher). People loved him and asked him to arbitrate in cases of dispute. Rabbi Ephraim Kutaner from Brodi met him then. The young man became his favorite. Rabbi Ephraim saw him often, admired him as a peacemaker, just and merciful. He offered Baal Shem his daughter in marriage. The Rabbi died very soon after that and Baal Shem went to Brodi to see the girl's bother, Rabbi Abraham Gershom Kutaner, a well-known talmudist and kabbalist. The young man made the worst impression on him: a poor peasant-clad *am-haaretz*, a rustic ignoramus: the haughty scholar would not allow such an alliance! But Hannah, Rabbi Ephraim's daughter, accepted the young stranger at once and insisted that her father's will be honored. Rabbi Abraham had to yield. On one condition: they would leave Brodi and go to live far away. They went to live in the wilderness of the Carpathian mountians, as lime-diggers among non-Jewish villagers. For seven years, twice a week, Israel would load their cart with lime, which Hannah would sell to the villagers. Very poor and happy they were, so legend would have it. Israel could have enough leisure to meditate, to study and to contemplate the majesty of nature. From the mountain folk he learned the curative virtues of herbs. After the seven years they decided to return to populous centers. In a neighboring village Hannah's brother bought them a small inn, of which Hannah, the faithful and understanding wife, took care; Israel, alone in a hut by the river Pruth, would spend days studying and meditating.

At the age of thirty-six he decided to "reveal" himself. His reputation as a travelling healer—healer of the soul and the body—grew. With Hannah and their two children, Hershel and Adel, they moved in 1740 to the town of Medzibor in Podolia. He ceased to travel so frequently. People came to him. In 1760 Baal Shem died.

For Baal Shem Tov and his true followers no absolute and static demarcation between good and evil, between sacred and profane, exists. "Nothing in him is eschatological," says Martin Buber in *The Origin and Meaning of Hasidism*, Vol. II of *Hasidism and the Way of Man*, ed. and tr. Maurice Friedman (New York: Horizon Press, 1960). ". . . Nowhere do we hear 'I have come in order to. . . .'", pp. 39–40.

"'What do you advise me to do with my son, he is a real *rasha* (villain),' asked a despairing father. 'Love him all the more,' advised the Baal Shem. 'God dwelleth with them in the midst of their uncleanliness.'" (Rabinowicz, p. 30.) "'I hope,'" the Besht is reported to have said one day, "'I can love a tsaddik [a community leader outstanding for his faith and piety] as much as God loves a wicked man.'" Jerome R. Mintz, *Legends of the Hasidim* (Chicago: University of Chicago Press, 1968), p. 169.

A true Hassid "cannot serve God merely by avoiding evil," comments Martin Buber, ". . . Sparks of God's light, in their deepest exile we call evil, yearn for liberation. Burdened with their shells . . . they come to us as 'alien thoughts,' as desires . . . but God is in them." *Hasidism*, Vol. II, pp. 53, 54.

Baal Shem Tov never committed his thoughts to writing. His was an oral communication. It was the role of his two beloved disciples and closest friends, the learned Rabbis Dov Baer, Maggid (preacher) of Meseritz, and Jacob Joseph of Polona, to establish the philosophical-theological foundations of the nascent Hassidism.

7. As quoted in Buber, p. 53.

8. Rabbi Nachman of Bratislaw: Born in 1772, son of Feige, the daughter of Baal Shem's (see note 6 of Chapter 2), beloved daughter Adel. Feige the Hassida was "said to be endowed with 'divine spirit.' It was her influence, rather than that of her husband, Rabbi Simcha, that inspired her illustrious son." Rabinowicz, p. 105.

Since childhood Nachman was a passionate and assiduous student of the Talmud and the Kabbalah. "What Yehuda Halevi (1085–1140) achieved in poetry, Rabbi Nachman expressed in prose. He produced many memorable aphorisms." (Rabinowicz, pp. 64–65.) Unshakable faith and the joy in and of it was the foundation of his inner life. Despised philosophy—even criticized Maimonides. Despised medical

profession, had contempt for any form of wealth and any form of ostentation. Foe of the *zaddiks* of his time.

"Once he spent the night in a newly-built wooden cabin and slumber fled from his eyes. 'I could not close my eyes all night,' he related next morning. 'I felt the groaning of the timbers. They wailed and moaned, because they had been cut off before their time.'" Rabinowicz, *ibid.*

Since early youth he had been longing for the Holy Land. In 1798, frail and poor, against the will of his family, he went there. Returned in 1799, full of enthusiasm, and continued longing to go back again during the rest of his short life. Died in 1812. "Make me worthy to serve thee"—was one of his prayers—"with a pure and unaffected faith . . . save me, as well as all thy people Israel, from the probing and searching intellect." [Source not retrieved. E. W.]

9. Rabbi Dov Baer, called the Maggid of Meseritz (1710–1772). Learned talmudist and student of theoretical Kabbalah. Of poor health, went to see Baal Shem to look for a cure. Found a teacher and a friend. After death of the Besht became his successor and missionary, settled in the town of Meseritz, which became the center of the first Hassidic masters. Formulator of Hassidic philosophy.

10. Zaddik: a person outstanding for his piety and faith. Hassidic *rebbe*, the community's socio-

religious leader. ". . . the man who leads the community in God's place," comments Buber (p. 41). Community as "both the definite limited community of this individual zaddik and the community of all Israel." (*Ibid.*) The zaddik was the Torah: "In the way he tied and untied his sandals was represented that in the Torah which is inexpressible but . . . can be transmitted through human existence." *Ibid.*, p. 43.

11. Mintz, *Legends*, p. 178.

12. Rabinowicz, p. 66.

13. Bet ha-midrash: a school for higher rabbinical studies, often attached to a synagogue. A "study center where people assembled to listen to . . . exposition of the Law from very early in the Second Temple period." *Ency. Jud.*, Vol. 4, p. 751.

14. Mishna: "earliest codification of Jewish Oral Law." Also "*Mishnah* (pl. *mishnayot*), subdivision of tractates of the Mishnah." *Ency. Jud.*, Vol. 11, Glossary. Together, *Gemara* and *Mishna* form the Talmud.

15. Zohar: *Sefer Ha Zohar: The Book of Radiance*, or, *of Splendor*. The Zohar, a collection of several books (in its complete printed form, five volumes) of short kabbalistic interpretations of the Torah and "longer homilies . . . in which Rabbi Simeon ben Yohai, a famous teacher [*tanna*] of the 2nd century, and his friends and students interpret the words of Scripture in accordance with their hidden meaning, and, moreover, almost always in the Aramaic language." Gershom G. Scholem,

Zohar, The Book of Splendor; Basic Readings from the Kabbalah (5th ed., New York: Schocken Books, 1971), p. 10.

Written largely between 1280 and 1286 by Moses b. Shem Tov de Leon. "The Zohar is the most important evidence of the survival of mystical spirit in medieval Judaism." *Ency. Jud.*, "The Zohar," Vol. 10, pp. 532–33.

The aim of the book was "to attack the literal conception of Judaism, the neglect of the performances of the *mitzwot* [pl. of *mitzvah*, "biblical or rabbinic injunction; applied also to good or charitable deeds"; *Ency. Jud.*, Vol. 11, Glossary], and emphasizing the supreme value and secret meaning of every word and command of the Torah." *Ibid.* p. 533.

"The main part of the Zohar, which is arranged by Pentateuch portions, purports to be an ancient Midrash [see note 6 to Chapter 3], and in many details it imitates the form of the ancient midrashic works of the first centuries C. E. . . ." Scholem, *Zohar*, p. 11.

". . . The whole corpus of Zohar literature was in origin made up of three strata. These, in themselves predominantly unified, are:

1) *Midrash ha-Neelam.* [The secret Midrash.]

2) The main part of the Zohar with the *Idra Rabba* [the Great Assembly], *Idra Zutta* [the Small Assembly], *Sitre Torah* [Secrets of the Torah] and most of the other short treatises.

3) *Raya Mehemna* [the Faithful Shepherd: Moses] and the so-

called *Tikkune Zohar*, both of which had a single author.

"Certain it is that the author of the third stratum, who had the second before him in completed form and cites it . . . is not the author of the first two. . . . This last [the third] group . . . was composed around 1300.

"The first two strata, on the other hand, are in all probability by a single author. . . ." (Scholem, pp. 14–15). These main parts of Zohar were composed around 1280 by Moses de Leon (died in 1305).

16. *Ibid.*, p. 70.

17. *Ibid.*, p. 33.

18. *Ibid.*, p. 82.

19. See under *Kether*, in note 12 to Chapter 3.

20. Rabbi Elijah ben Salomon, the Gaon of Vilna (*Ency. Jud.*, Vol. 7, pp. 315–23). Gaon (Excellence, pl. Geonim), "formal title of the heads of the academies of Sura and Pumbedita in Babylonia . . . from the end of the sixth century or somewhat later to the middle of the 11th. . . ." (*Ibid.*, p. 315.) Later it became an honorific title for any rabbi or anyone with great knowledge of Torah. The Geonim were considered the intellectual leaders of the entire *Diaspora.* The Gaon of Vilna was considered the greatest Halakhic (legal Judaism's) authority of eastern European Jewry. Born in Vilna (the capital of Lithuania) in 1720. Never diverged from the path of Torah. Studied Hebrew grammar, mathematics, biology, medicine. Also studied and commented on classical Kabbalah. Mystic, he nevertheless became the greatest adversary of nascent Hassidism. Two decades of battle. The Hassidic disregard of strict obedience to the minutiae of rabbinical regulations, the Hassidic cult of zaddikism, were horror to him. In 1792 with the consent of the Gaon, the elders of Vilna issued a *cherem* (decree of excommunication) against the "Godless" sect. The Gaon died in 1797.

21. Hassidism (*Ency. Jud.*, Vol. 7, pp. 1390–1432). "A popular religious movement . . . which emerged in Judaism and Jewry in the second half of the 18th century. [Its founder: Israel Baal Shem Tov (the Besht); see note 6 to Chapter 2.] Ecstasy, mass enthusiasm, close-knit group cohesion, and charismatic leadership [the Hassidic cult of the zaddik, the Hassidic community leader, a cult that led to the establishment of powerful and often abusive dynasties of famous zaddiks] . . . are the distinguishing socioreligious marks of Ḥasidism." *Ibid.*, p. 1390.

"The movement began in the extreme southeast of Poland-Lithuania, and was shaped and conditioned by the tension prevailing in Jewish society . . . created by the breakup of Poland-Lithuania in the late 18th century and the three partitions of the country. This combined with the problems inherited as a result of . . . the Chmielnicki massacres [Cossack uprising led by Chmielnicki in the middle of the seventeenth century]. . . . The framework of Jewish leadership was shaken, and the authority and methods of Jewish leaders were further undermined and questioned in the wake of the upheaval brought about by the false messianic and kabbalistic movements of Shabbetai Zevi [in the sixties of the seventeenth century] and Jacob Frank, the shadow of the latter lying on Hasidism from its inception." *Ibid.*, p. 1391.

22. See Jaffa Eleach, "The Russian dissenting sects and their influence on Israel Baal Shem Tov, founder of Hassidism," *Proceedings of the American Academy for Jewish Research*, 36 (1968), 72.

23. *Shtetle*: Jewish small-town community in Eastern Europe.

24. *Mitzvah*: biblical or rabbinic injunction; applied also to good or charitable deeds.

25. See my *Fragments of Life, Metaphysics and Art* (New York: The Bond Wheelwright Co., 1953) p. xi.

26. See Scholem, *Zohar*, pp. 96–97.

27. Chaim Soutine (1894–1943), born in Lithuania.

28. Scholem, p. 72.

29. *Ibid.*, p. 115.

30. *Ibid.*, p. 34–35.

3. The Road of Meditation

1. Paul Klee, *Pedagogical Sketchbook*, Introduction and translation by Sibyl Moholy-Nagy (New York: Frederick A. Praeger, 1953; original German, 1925), p. 53.

2. See note 6, below.

3. "Merkabah mysticism or 'Ma'-aseh Merkavah,' the name given to the first chapter of Ezekiel in *Mishnah Hagigah*, 2:1. The term was used by the rabbis to designate the complex of speculations, homilies, and visions connected with the Throne of Glory and the chariot (*merkavah*) which bears it and all that is embodied in this divine world. . . . This was a study surrounded by a special holiness and a special danger. . . . Therefore the rabbis sought to conceal the Book of Ezekiel." *Ency. Jud.*, Vol. 11, p. 1386.

Merkabah mysticism is "the first phase in the development of Jewish mysticism before its crystallization in the mediaeval Kabbalah . . . also the longest. Its literary remains [the so-called "Hekhaloth Books," i.e., descriptions of the *hekhaloth*, the heavenly halls or palaces, stages of soul's "ascension" to the Chariot] are traceable over a period of almost a thousand years, from the first century B.C. to the tenth A.D." Scholem: *Major Trends in Jewish Mysticism* (New York: Schocken Books, 1954), p. 40.

". . . the earliest Jewish mysticism is throne-mysticism. Its essence is not absorbed contemplation of God's true nature, but perception of His appearance on the throne, as described by Ezekiel, and cognition of the mysteries of the celestial throne-world. The throne-world is to the Jewish mystic what the *pleroma*, the 'fullness,' the bright sphere of divinity with its potencies, aeons, archons and dominions is to the

Hellenistic and early Christian mystics of the period who appear in the history of religion under the names of Gnostics and Hermetics. The Jewish mystic . . . nevertheless expresses his vision in terms of his own religious background. God's pre-existing throne, which embodies and exemplifies all forms of creation, is at once the goal and the theme of his mystical vision. . . .

"The outstanding documents of the movement [Merkabah] appear to have been edited in the fifth and sixth centuries when its spirit was still alive and vigorous." *Ibid.*, p. 44.

This Merkabah spirit was rekindled later, in the eleventh and twelfth centuries in Italy and the Rhineland, whence it spread to thirteenth-century southern France and Spain.

4. Hasidei Ashkenaz. See "Kabbalah," by G. G. Scholem, *Ency. Jud.*, Vol. 10, p. 514.

5. Rabbi Jacob Joseph of Polona. Along with Rabbi Dov Baer (the Maggid of Meseritz), he was the beloved disciple and friend of Baal Shem. (See end of notes 6 and 9 of Chapter 2.) Very erudite in Halakhah, Talmud, and Kabbalah. Before his conversion to Hassidism he was hostile to the concept of "popular *rebbe.*" He became the first theoretician of Hassidism. He died in 1782.

6. *Midrash*: the "method of interpreting Scripture to elucidate legal points (*Midrash Halakhah*) or to bring out lessons by stories or homiletics (*Midrash Aggadah*).

Also the name for a collection of such rabbinic interpretations [*Midrashim*]." (*Ency. Jud.*, Vol. 11, Glossary). Halakhah (from "to go") is the legal side of Judaism as distinct from the non-legal material of rabbinic literature. *Halakhah* (pl. *halakhot*) originally meant a particular law or decision in a given moment. In Talmud, the word of the Lord means *Halakhah. Halakhot* is the legal and ritual system of Judaism.

During the first two centuries A.D.—the era of the *tannaim*, the "teachers"—*halakhah*, the traditional Oral Law's material, immensely accrued, was assembled by them, codified, and edited into what became the basic content of the Talmud, the so-called Mishna, the final completion of which is ascribed traditionally to the second-century Rabbi Judah ben Nasi. Just as the existing *halakhoth* were collected in Mishna, so the much larger *aggadhic* material (narrative—ethical, poetical) was gathered in the *Midrashim* (sixth-seventh to tenth century). Now, as the discussions of the Oral Law (*Halakhah*) led up to the Mishna, the Mishna itself became the subject of further discussions, interpretations and enlargements.

This immense material, both *halakhic* and *aggadhic*, was written down and named *Gemara* (=to learn completely), the two together constituting the *Talmud* (="teaching," instructing)—the creative achievement of the scholars called *amoraim* (third to fifth century A.D.), who succeeded the order of *tannaim* in both Palestine and Babylonia. (The Palestinian Talmud, a compendium of the discussions and decisions of the Palestinian sages, and the Babylonian Talmud, much larger, the creative work of the Babylonian Academies.)

Haggadic (*Aggadah* or *Haggadah* in Hebrew narration): "an amplification of those portions of the Bible which include narrative, history, ethical maxims, and the reproofs and consolations of the prophets. . . ." *Ency. Jud.*, Vol. 2, p. 354.

"The *aggadah*, in common with the *halakhah* [religious laws and relations] is part of the literature of the Oral Law. . . ." *Ibid.*

"The *aggadah* is first and foremost the creation of Palestinian Jewry, from the time of the Second Temple to the end of the talmudic period. . . ." *Ibid.*, p. 356.

"The older works of the *aggadah* are also the most ancient sources of Jewish mysticism." *Ibid.*, p. 361.

7. Louis Sullivan, quoted by Siegfried Giedion, *Space, Time and Architecture* (3rd ed., Cambridge: Harvard University Press, 1954), p. 413.

8. Rabbi Shneur Zalman of Lyady, in Bielo-Russia (1745–1813). His scrupulous and solid erudition not only as a talmudist and classical kabbalist, but as a student of mathematics, astronomy and Hebrew grammar, rivaled that of the great Gaon of Vilna, his foe (see note 20 of Chapter 2). Founder of an Hassidic movement, the so-

called "Habad" Hassidism, a synthesis of strict halakhic content and kabbalistic speculation. Founder also of the Lubavich dynasty of zaddiks.

9. [From a popular illustrated weekly or monthly magazine lent to Léo by me at the time of its publication. Efforts to retrieve this source have failed. E. W.]

10. *Zimzum*: "The basic source of this doctrine is found in an early fragment from the circle of the *Sefer-ha-Iyyun* [twelfth–thirteenth century?] which speaks of an act of divine contraction that preceded emanations: 'How did He produce and create this world? Like a man who gathers in and contracts (*mezamzem*) his breath [Shem Tov. b. Shem Tov has, "and contracts Himself"], so that the smaller might contain the larger, so He contracted His light into a hand's breadth, according to his own measure. . . .'" Scholem, *Ency. Jud.*, Vol. 10, pp. 588–89.

11. Luria, Isaak ben Salomon (1534–1572), called Ha-Ari, the [sacred] Lion; the most famous and influential kabbalist in modern times; founder of the so-called Lurianic Kabbalah. His father emigrated from Germany or Poland to Jerusalem. As a child he was taken to Egypt, where he was initiated in the esoteric studies. Established in Safed, he continued his studies, both halakhic and cabbalistic, under the guidance of the illustrious Rabbi Moses b. Cordovero (note 13, below), the greatest dialectician of theoretical Kabbalah. After the death of his teacher in

1570, Luria became the head of the Safed school. His teaching—exclusively oral—was assembled, summarized and commented on by some of his most outstanding and creative disciples, Hayyim Vital and Israel Sarug (note 15, below) in particular.

12. *Sefirot*: "The . . . metaphysical 'numbers' or 'numerations' of the divine aspects, are the principal keys [in Kabbalah] to the mysteries of the Torah. They form a tenfold hierarchy, and their names, enumerated from the highest downward, are: . . ." See Schaya, *The Universal Meaning of the Kabbalah*, "Contemplation of the Divine Aspects," pp. 21–60, from which this entire footnote is taken.

1) *Kether*, crown, "*Kether*, in its pure and absolute essence, has no aspects; it is the eternally mysterious reality: . . ." "Thus, the Kabbalah calls *kether* in itself: *ain*, 'nothingness,'. . . non-being or super-being, non-cause . . . ; *en sof*, 'no end,' infinite. . . ." *Ibid.*, p. 36.

2) *Hokhmah*, "'wisdom,' or the *first* divine emanation [italics mine] . . . *Hokhmah* is also called *mahshabah*, which signifies 'thought,' 'meditation' and also 'art.'. . ." *Ibid.*, p. 39.

3) *Binah*, "the revelatory and creative 'intelligence.'. . . God contemplates himself in *binah*, the universal 'mother,' as the One in the multiple. . . ." *Ibid.*, p. 43.

4) *Hesed*, God's "'grace,' 'greatness,' 'charity,' 'God's love.'" *Ibid.*, pp. 46–47.

5) *Din*, "judgement,' also 'power,' or 'fear.'" *Ibid.*, p. 21.

6) *Tifereth*, "God's 'beauty,'" God's "infinite unity in so far as it is revealed as the plenitude and blissful harmony of all his possibilities. . . . God's 'heart' or 'compassion.'" *Ibid.*, pp. 49–50.

7) *Netsah*, "'victory' or . . . 'constancy' . . . 'perpetuity.'" *Ibid.*, note 1, p. 56.

8) *Hod*, God's "'glory' . . . 'majesty.'" *Ibid.*, p. 21.

9) *Yesod*, God's "'foundation' (or *tsedek*, 'justice')." *Ibid.*, pp. 21, 56 note 2.

10) The last *Sefirah*, *Malkhuth*, "the 'kingdom' of God, which produces, encircles and penetrates the whole of creation. . . ." *Ibid.*, p. 57. She is the end that joins the beginning, the Shekhinah, the Presence, the "lower mother" as she is called.

"All the *Sefiroth* 'descend' from *kether*, in perfect co-emanation and co-operation, and are finally concentrated in *malkhuth* and manifested by *malkhuth*. . . ." *Ibid.*, p. 59.

And so ". . . the tenfold unity of the *Sefiroth* is shown as a hierarchy of three triads projected into their common recipient, namely, the tenth and last *Sefirah*, *malkhuth*, which is the immediate cause of the cosmos. The highest triad, *kether-hokhmah-binah* (crown-wisdom-intelligence), is that of the essential and ontological principles; the second triad, *hesed-din-tifereth* (grace-judgement-beauty), is that of the cosmological principles; the third, *netsah-hod-yesod* (victory-glory-foundation), is that of the cosmic powers and the creative act; finally, the *Sefirah*, *malkhuth* (kingdom) . . . is the uncreated and creative substance, or . . . divine immanence. Elsewhere, these four Sefirothic degrees are respectively the archetypes of the 'four worlds' of transcendent 'emanation,' prototypical 'creation,' subtle 'formation,' and sensory 'fact'." *Ibid.*, pp. 30–31.

13. Cordovero, Moses ben Jacob (1522–1570), birthplace unknown, but name testifies to Spanish origin. He was a teacher of Isaac Luria. Wrote various commentaries, including one on the Zohar. All of his work is "a major attempt to synthesize and to construct a speculative kabbalistic system. . . . done especially in his theology, which is based on the Zohar. . . ." See *Ency. Jud.* Vol. 5, pp. 967–70.

14. Breaking of the Vessels: seven of them broke; the first upper group of three remained integral. The detailed account-résumé of this primeval Drama as well as of all other historical and epistemological related aspects, speculative facts and visions of Kabbalah can be found in the excellent, competent and careful study by Gershom Scholem in *Ency. Jud.*, Vol. 10, pp. 490ff. My attentive and *repeated* reading of this work became a basic and sufficient sup-

port to my own meditation on this subject.

15. Sarug, Israel (fl. 1590–1610), Egyptian kabbalist. "Sarug may have known Isaac Luria while the latter was in Egypt . . . later claimed to be one of his main disciples." See biography in *Ency. Jud.*, Vol. 14, pp. 889–90.

16. See Yaffa Eleach (above, note 22 of Chapter 2), pp. 79–80. Quoted by permission of the American Academy for Jewish Research.

17. Parzufim: configurations "(literally 'faces') . . . now take the place of the *Sefirot* as the principal manifestations of *Adam Kadmon*." Scholem, *Ency. Jud.*, Vol. 10, p. 598.

18. "This 'coupling' is aroused by the reascent of the 288 sparks that had been in the broken vessels and returned to the bowels of *Binah*, where they play the role of animating and quickening forces within a structure whose function is primarily receptive. Without such assisting forces, which are referred to as 'female waters' . . . there can be neither 'coupling' nor unification even in the world of *azilut* [emanation]. From the union of *Abba* and *Imma* a new *parzuf* is born, known as *Ze'eir Anpin* (literally, 'the short-faced one,' i.e., 'the impatient' or 'unindulgent one'), which is comprised of the six lower *Sefirot*. . . . Here we have the center for the cathartic processes that take place in all the *parzufim* in order to mitigate the harsh powers of *Din*; their ultimate success depends on a long,

almost endless series of developments. . . . The last and tenth *Sefirah*, *Malkhut*, is also converted into a *parẓuf*, which is named *Nukba de-Ze'eir*, 'the female of Ze-eir,' and represents the latter's complementary feminine aspect. . . .

"The five principal *parẓufim* of *Abba*, *Imma*, *Arikh Anpin*, *Ze'eir Anpin*, and *Nukba de-Ze'eir* constitute the figure of the *Adam Kadmon* as it evolves in the first stages of *tikkun*." *Ibid.*, pp. 599–600.

19. *Yod*: see note 3 of Chapter 1.
20. Hasidei Ashkenaz: see note 4 of Chapter 3.
21. With a few changes introduced by me in quoting myself, the following passages are from *Five Variations*, pp. 142, 63–65.
22. Persian mystic Junayd (ninth–tenth century), quoted in E. G. Browne, *A Literary History of Persia* (Cambridge, England: Cambridge University Press, 1928), Vol. I, p. 427.
23. Bronstein, note 21 above.
24. *Ibid.*, p. 189.
25. Bronstein, "Romantic Homage to Greece and Spain. My Fable, Their Art" (typescript), p. 106.
26. The following is quoted with slight changes by me from *Five Variations*, pp. 41–42.
27. Charles W. Hendel, introduction to Ernest Cassirer, *The Philosophy of Symbolic Forms*, Vol. I (New Haven: Yale University Press, 1953).
28. Bronstein, *Five Variations*, pp. 41–42.

29. *Ibid.*, p. 164 (slightly altered by me).
30. *Ibid.*, p. 40.
31. Paul Klee, p. 56.
32. *Ibid.*, p. 53.
33. *Ibid.*, p. 54.
34. *Ibid.*, p. 57.
35. *Ibid.*, p. 60.
36. *The Diaries of Paul Klee, 1898–1918*, ed., with an introduction, by Felix Klee (Berkeley and Los Angeles: University of California Press, 1964), p. 239, tr. of entry 863 (Munich, 1909), *Klee-Tagebücher* (Copyright © DuMont Buchverlag, Cologne, 1968). Used courtesy Felix Klee.

> *Öffne Dich, Du Pforte in der Tiefe,*
> *Verlies im Grunde, gib mich frei,*
> *den Belichtung Witternden.*
> *Und helle Hände kommen, die mich greifen,*
> *Und Freundes Worte sagen froh:*
> *Her ihr Bilder schöner, wilder Tiere,*
> *entsteiget Eurem Zwinger,*
> *dass lieblich gleiten Finger durch flammend Fell.*
> *Und eins ist man wie ehedem in Gottes Garten:*
> *Tag und Nacht und Sonn' und Pracht der Sterne.*
> *(Im Paradies der Dichtung-Zitternden.)*

E. W. Suggests:

> *Open, you deep-down gate,*
> *Underground dungeon, set me free,*

who scent a lighting of light.
And bright hands come, that
grasp me,
and, happy, the words of a
friend say:
Come, you pictures of wild
beasts in their beauty,
rise from your prison,
that fingers may glide sweet
through flaming fell.
And we are one as of old in
God's garden:
day and night
and sun and splendor of the
stars.
(In the paradise of those who
tremble with poetry.)

4. The Road of Companions

1. Scholem, *Ency. Jud.*, Vol. 10, p. 514.
2. Bronstein, *Fragments*, p. 52.
3. Giovanni di Paolo (*ca.* 1400–*ca.* 1482), Italian painter, born and lived all his life in Siena. The first mention of his name is in 1423. The influential Sienese painters of his formative years were Paolo di Giovanni Fei, Taddeo di Bartolo, Sassetta, Gentile da Fabriano. Long neglected, he is now seen as a great and original master; Berenson called him the "El Greco of the Quattrocento"; the terms *expressionism* and even *surrealism* have been used in describing his art. See *Praeger Encyclopedia of Art* (New York, Washington, London: Praeger, 1971.)
4. Bronstein, *Fragments*, p. 133.
5. See note 20 to Chapter 1.
6. *Ibid.*
7. See note 2 to Chapter 1.
8. Attribution of the Camera delle Cariatidi to Dosso Dossi has been questioned. Among the authorities who give it to Dosso are Berenson and Felton Gibbons.
9. The King James version of the Bible, John 2 : 1–5. In the *New English Bible with the Apocrypha*, The New Testament, John 2, Christ the Giver of Life (London: Oxford University Press, Cambridge University Press, 1970), the passage is translated:

> *On the third day there was a wedding at Cana-in-Galilee. The mother of Jesus was there, and Jesus and his disciples were guests also. The wine gave out, so Jesus's mother said to him, "They have no wine left." He answered, "Your concern, Mother, is not mine. My hour has not yet come." His mother said to the servants, "Do whatever he tells you."*

Credits

Permission to reprint the following texts has been received from:

American Academy for Jewish Research, New York: passages from Jaffa Eleach, "The Russian Dissenting Sects and their Influence on Israel Baal Shem Tov, Founder of Hassidism," in *The Proceedings* (Volume XXXVI, 1968)

A. S. Barnes Co., Inc., Cranbury, N.J.: passages from Dr. H. Rabinowicz, *A Guide to Hassidism* (1960)

Basil Blackwell, Oxford, England: passages from Ludwig Wittgenstein, *Philosophical Investigations* (1967)

DuMont Buchverlag, Cologne, Germany: the original text, entry 863, *Klee-Tagebücher* (c/1968 DuMont Buchverlag)

Macmillan Co., Jerusalem-New York, *Encyclopedia Judaica, passim*

Horizon Press, New York: passages from Martin Buber, *The Origins and Meaning of Hasidism* (copyright 1960 Horizon Press)

Felix Klee, Switzerland: permission to use the Eleanor Wolff translation of entry 863, *Klee-Tagebücher*

Hattula Moholy-Nagy, Switzerland: passages from Paul Klee, *Pedagogical Sketchbook*

Polish Institute of Arts and Sciences in America, New York: Watson Kirkconnell's translation of the first lines of *Pan Tadeusz by Adam Mickiewicz*

120
Credits

Schocken Books, Inc., New York: Passages from Gershom G. Scholem, *Zohar: The Book of Splendor* (Copyright © 1949; copyright renewed © 1977 by Schocken Books, Inc.). Also passages from Gershom G. Scholem, *Major Trends in Jewish Mysticism* (Copyright 1946, © 1954 by Schocken Books, Inc. Copyright renewed © 1974 by Schocken Books, Inc.)

Lyle Stuart, New York: Passages from Leon Schaya, *The Universal Meaning of the Kabbalah* (Copyright © 1971 by George Allen and Unwin Ltd. Printed by arrangement with Lyle Stuart)

University of California Press, Berkeley: the poem entry 863 from *The Diaries of Paul Klee 1898–1918*, ed. with an introduction by Felix Klee (Copyright © 1964 by The Regents of the University of California).

Library of Congress Cataloging in Publication Data

Bronstein, Léo.
  Kabbalah and art.

  Includes bibliographical references.
   1. Art—Psychology—Addresses, essays, lectures.
  2. Cabala—Addresses, essays, lectures.
  3. Hasidism—Addresses, essays, lectures.
  I. Title.
N71.B77   701'.15   78-63585
ISBN 0-87451-163-1

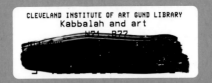